Making It Happen

Creating Success
and Abundance

ESSENCE
BOOKS

MAKING IT HAPPEN

CREATING SUCCESS AND ABUNDANCE

Edited by PATRICIA M. HINDS
Introduction by ED LEWIS

ESSENCE
BOOKS

Time Inc. Home Entertainment

President: Rob Gursha
Vice-president, New Product Development: Richard Fraiman
Executive Director, Marketing Services: Carol Pittard
Director, Retail & Special Sales: Tom Mifsud
Director of Finance: Tricia Griffin
Marketing Director: Ann Marie Doherty
Prepress Manager: Emily Rabin
Associate Book Production Manager: Suzanne Janso

Special thanks: Bozena Bannett, Alexandra Bliss, Bernadette Corbie, Robert Dente, Anne-Michelle Gallero, Peter Harper, Robert Marasco, Natalie McCrea, Jonathan Polsky, Margarita Quiogue, Mary Jane Rigoroso, Steven Sandonato, Grace Sullivan

Time Inc.
1271 Avenue of the Americas
New York, New York 10020

ISBN: 1-932273-57-3
Library of Congress control number: 2004108519

We welcome your comments and suggestions about Essence books. Please write to us at:
Essence Books
Attention: Book Editors
P.O. Box 11016
Des Moines, IA 50336-1016

If you would like to order any of our hardcover Collector's Edition books, please call us at (800) 327-6388 (Monday through Friday, 7:00 A.M.–8:00 P.M., or Saturday, 7:00 A.M.–6:00 P.M. Central Time).

CONTRIBUTORS

Editor-in-Chief: Patricia M. Hinds

Writers: Tomika Anderson, Kenya Byrd, Joy Duckett Cain, Nana Eyeson, Deborah Gregory, Tracy Hopkins, Sherri McGee, Diane Patrick, Jenyne Raines

Editorial Assistant: Tauheedah Muhammad

Designer: Elizabeth Van Itallie

Contributing Editors: Sharon Boone, Alison France, Rosemarie Robotham

Copy Editors: Nana Badu, Maxine Bartow, Sherrill Clarke

Interviewer: Cassidy Arkin

Photo Researcher: Monique Valeris

Administrative Assistant: Kameela Abdul-Maajid

Interns: Pamela Jackson, Bridget Jefferys, Julia McClure

Produced and packaged by Mignon Communications

Special thanks: Susan L. Taylor, Marlowe Goodson, Diane Weathers, Jan deChabert, Cheryl Fenton, Sandra Martin, Lena Sherrod, Fred Allen, Jean Borrie, Karen Brown, Denolyn Carroll, Adriane Carter, Faith Childs-Davis, Yvette Cutler, Monique Davis, Cynthia Gordy, Tamara Jeffries, Marsha Kelly, Sandra Lawrence, LaVon Leak-Wilks, Kathryn Leary, Jennelle Mahone-Sy, Kyissa Markland, Claire McIntosh, Christine Mekhail, Michael Morgan, Cori M. Murray, Jonell Nash, Debra Parker, Jackie Richardson, Danielle Robinson, Constance Robotham-Reid, Leah Rudolfo, Annette Simmons, Bryan Stair, Mikki Taylor, Linda Villarosa, Wilhelmenia Weston, Charlotte Wiggers, Darryl Wilson

Acknowledgments: Gregory Boyea, Edgerton Maloney, Paul Nocera, Larry Ramo, Seth Rappaport, Lisa Sorensen, Biff Warren

CONTENTS

Realizing a dream

Introduction by ED LEWIS

To quote my favorite poet Langston Hughes, "life for me ain't been no crystal stair." However, I learned a few things along the way that helped me achieve the business success I enjoy today.

I grew up in a rough neighborhood in the Bronx, New York. I lived in the projects with my mother, a beautician, and my father, a janitor. During my youth, I spent summers in Prince Edward County, Virginia, visiting my grandparents' farm—planting, plowing and harvesting the land. A strong work ethic and the importance of education were a major part of my upbringing.

I've always been a dreamer, and I wanted to follow my dream of becoming an entrepreneur. After receiving bachelor's and master's degrees from the University of New Mexico, I attended Georgetown Law School. But I wasn't destined to pursue law. I left Georgetown and secured an executive training position at First National City Bank, which later became Citibank. While there, I learned about finance and the importance of cash flow. I also reinforced my personal commitment to be the best, beginning my workday at 6:00 A.M. and working until 11:00 P.M.—six days a week, including some Sundays. I gained an understanding of the complex financial needs of corporations. Most important, I gained the self-confidence that flowed from preparation and hard work. Later I would realize that no experience is ever wasted.

There was, however, something nagging at me during my college years and my tenure at First National: I wanted to have something of my own. When I was a youngster, my uncle, a businessman, had often talked to me about the need to take control of your destiny. Thus, in 1968, I joined Clarence Smith and three other men to start a magazine for Black women.

Our vision was to provide something of value for the Black woman—a voice and sisterhood of support. In 1970, our first year of publishing ESSENCE, our circulation was 50,000; today it is more than 1,000,000. Indeed, ESSENCE has come a long way, mirroring the growth of African-American business over the past 35 years.

In 2004, we launched *Suede*, a new fashion-and-beauty magazine for young multicultural women. And for the past ten years, the Essence Music Festival has kicked off the July 4th weekend in New Orleans, attracting more than 200,000 people annually. Moreover, we have beautiful books, such as this one you are about to enjoy. All together, in 2004 the gross sales of Essence Communications will exceed $150 million.

But in order to accelerate our economic advancement as a community, we must make a stronger commitment to the growing number of Black entrepreneurs—women and men—and make sure we support their businesses, if merited. And I want Essence Communications to be as far-reaching as our corporate partner, Time Warner.

We have all come through a time of great uncertainty with renewed hope, caring and purpose. ESSENCE is a virtual community—a source of spiritual guidance, a leader of activism, a role model of achievement, a reflection of African-American beauty in all shapes, sizes and skin tones, and a voice for economic empowerment of African-American women.

MAKING IT HAPPEN

Foreword by PATRICIA M. HINDS

More than two decades ago I registered my business names, Mignon Creations and Mignon Communications. Back then, I was teaching, had completed my master's degree and had just seen my first children's book, *Animal Affairs,* published by Dell Publishing. Becoming an author was an incredibly life-changing experience. It began with a brief conversation with an editor who liked my idea. From there, I decided to try the publishing world full-time. After spending more than a year at Harper & Row Publishers, I knew much more about my talents and could see more clearly the direction in which I was headed. I realized that in working for a corporation, I would never reach the place I'd want to be—where I could call my own shots. Knowing this, I resolved to learn the skills and the business, storing the knowledge to be tapped in my own time and way.

At the time I wasn't quite sure what my business would be—probably something having to do with publishing or writing, creating educational books or producing and marketing a product. I had no firm plan; I was in no rush. But I saw a world of opportunities to pursue. My goal wasn't to own a multinational corporation—just to have something of my own. The *what, when* and *how* were not essential questions. I only knew *who* I'd become at some point in the future: an independent business person, embracing my life's calling.

In the years since, I've been blessed to be able to do things I love—create beautiful books for children and adults—and share knowledge that might inspire others. It's an art and a gift that I've been able to recognize and live. I've arrived at a place where fear of creating my own does not rule me—

faith does. I've seen some of my visions in my life, art and business become real, with many more still to be realized. And through teaching courses in entrepreneurship some years ago at New York University, I've seen others build on their desires.

This book is so much a reflection of a spirit I share with many of the entrepreneurs presented on these pages. They represent a diverse selection of businesspeople who live their passion and define prosperity on their own terms. The nature and size of their businesses vary immensely, but their minds are of common purpose—to be their own boss. They've set their goals, believed in themselves, pursued their dreams and passions. They have taken charge and made it happen. Some are wealthy in cash profits, others are less so, but all have benefited and are wealthy in terms of inner satisfaction. They have built something from a thought, a prayer, a desire to shape their own future. They have a sense of fulfillment that is immeasurable.

We've presented dynamic people who have found their niche as individuals, in family businesses or by becoming a brand in their own right. Some featured on these pages found a path to entrepreneurship after a challenge in life, some are sharing their wealth to make a difference in the lives of others, and still more have discovered the wonders of faith-based businesses. All of them embody a true spirit of entrepreneurship. These women and men are bold, smart visionaries. With the support of those who believe in them, they have been able to realize their vision of success and abundance. Through their stories, so many more may be inspired to take that leap of faith, to believe in a dream—and make it happen.

FINDING YOUR NICHE

"**B**elieve in yourself and have confidence that you can compete against all odds. Have a vision of what you'd like to accomplish and be able to articulate that vision."

—ROBERT JOHNSON

ROBERT JOHNSON

When opportunity knocked in 1979, Robert Johnson, founder and CEO of Black Entertainment Television, was there to open the door. He started BET, the first Black-owned cable network, with a $15,000 bank loan and $50,000 from an investor. In addition to BET, which he sold to Viacom in 2000 for $3 billion, Johnson's entrepreneurial spirit has led him to other business ventures. The nation's first Black billionaire, who once had equity in several magazines, owns several restaurants, nightclubs and a real-estate investment company. In 2003 the 57-year-old's hoop dreams came true when he purchased the Charlotte Bobcats, an NBA expansion franchise—making him the first African-American majority owner of a sports franchise.

RIGHT PLACE, RIGHT TIME

"Early on, I didn't feel I had the option of going to college. But I received a low-cost student loan and pursued a bachelor's degree in education, then graduate studies at Princeton."

CHANNEL SURFING

"I met someone in the Cable Trade Association, who offered me a job as a lobbyist. I recognized that there was an opportunity to create and deliver programming for African-Americans."

OBSTACLES ALONG THE WAY

"The principal obstacle I faced in launching BET was convincing cable operators to carry programming in markets across the country with small numbers of Black subscribers. It was also a challenge trying to convince advertisers that African-Americans buy the products they see and hear about in the media."

STAYING THE COURSE

"It's gratifying that I've seen my vision come to fruition. And it's even more important that the people who placed their trust in me—those who bought stock when BET was public or the people I've employed for many years—have benefited from my success. With BET, we have created more Black multimillionaires than any other company in America. And we have created opportunities for African-Americans to hold a variety of positions in the media."

OTHER VENTURES

"I also operate RLJ Development LLC, which includes a real-estate company that owns 11 hotels with a value of $250 million; Leeward Island's Lottery Holding Co., an online lottery company operating in six Caribbean countries; Ortanique Restaurants, a group of eateries featuring Caribbean-influenced cuisine; Wolverine Pizza restaurants in Detroit; BET Soundstage in Orlando; and Three Keys Music, a jazz recording company."

MAKING IT HAPPEN

"Believe in yourself and have confidence that you can compete against all odds. Have a vision of what you'd like to accomplish and be able to articulate that vision. Show leadership and the ability to direct and guide people. Demonstrate that you are willing to work as hard for your success as they are."

JACQUELINE JACKSON

Raising a child on a single-parent income is always difficult. In 2000, for Jacqueline Jackson, a high-school career coordinator, divorce meant that she'd have to support herself and her 6-year-old daughter on her teacher's salary. After ten years of working for Chicago's public schools, Jackson stumbled upon real estate. Four years ago the Chi-Town native purchased a condo for investment. Today the 40-year-old entrepreneur owns six multifamily units—with plans for more. She's working feverishly to become one of Chicago's real-estate titans.

SURVIVAL OF THE FITTEST

"After my divorce, I decided to become an entrepreneur. I was very concerned about raising my daughter on my teacher's salary, so I started looking for ways to supplement my income. A friend of mine worked in the pharmaceutical industry, and he invested in real estate on the side. He encouraged me to pursue it."

FIRST BUY

"To buy my first condo I used equity from my home to help with my credit and down payment. Also the seller paid part of the closing costs, which reduced my cash outlay."

MOVING ON UP

"After starting with a condo, I decided to invest in multifamily units. I found an empty building, but then I learned that most banks don't finance multifamily units. I was referred to ShoreBank, where the vice-president overcame his apprehension and extended a loan of $250,000 to me. Two weeks later every unit was occupied. Rental income was $5,000 a month, and my mortgage was $1,900. So there was a profit right off the top. Today because of the opportunity afforded me by ShoreBank, I volunteer with its community outreach program, mentoring young entrepreneurs."

DOING THE WORK

"When you buy real estate, many sellers are willing to pay closing costs, but you must ask. I negotiate the price on everything. I've found my passion, and I'm just trying to be the next Donald Trump."

CREDIT IS KEY

"I always advise my friends and tenants to start by cleaning up their credit. Once your credit is okay, you can find a way to make an investment. You don't have to be rich, inherit money or have your daddy give it to you. You can actually get it on your own. It's also important to have some savings."

READING IS FUNDAMENTAL

"I carry real-estate books with me everywhere. People always teased me about reading real-estate books as opposed to novels, but it has paid off. The bookstore is my best friend. I go there as often as some would go out to dinner or a movie."

MAKING IT HAPPEN

"You have to have faith. With faith comes confidence. There's enough real estate for everybody. Make sure you build a close relationship with a good bank, because bankers will work with you if they believe in you. You don't earn that overnight."

DAWN HAYNES

When wardrobe stylist and designer Dawn Haynes was laid off from a sales position at a sporting goods store, she vowed never to put herself at risk again. Today, not only does she have her own Los Angeles styling agency—called Dawn to Dusk—but she also has a $500,000 annual income and a Rolodex packed with the digits of some of Hollywood's brightest stars. A long way from selling sweats and socks, she is peddling high-end fashion very successfully.

THE BIG PAYBACK

"I was laid off from a job once because I was late too often. It was a humiliating experience that made me understand the importance of timeliness, but I never wanted to have to answer to anyone again. In 1991, launching my own business, I became the person in charge. Now, in addition to styling such celebrities as Eve, The Rock and Serena Williams, I negotiate business terms on behalf of hairstylists, makeup artists and photographers in New York, Los Angeles and other cities. Fortunately, I was able to turn a painful situation into a successful one."

CLEANING UP HER ACT

"I have wanted to be an entrepreneur since I was 10 years old. My first business was a car wash. Whenever my family hosted Thanksgiving dinners or other big parties, I washed all my relatives' cars. I hired my cousins to do all the work. Later I ran a yacht-cleaning business in Playa Del Rey, California, where I was raised. I would get $1,000 just to clean a specialized area of wood on each yacht. By the time I was 15, I knew that getting big checks and being able to hire people by the hour was what I wanted to do."

STYLING THE STARS

"When I was growing up, one of singer Teena Marie's bodyguards was a friend of mine. Teena really liked my fashion sense, so she asked me to become her stylist. I started touring with Teena in 1985, which led to my touring with Prince, Patti LaBelle and Sheila E. The opportunities to work with celebrities grew, and before I knew it, I was in business."

MOST DEFINING MOMENTS

"Working with Halle Berry was one of the biggest moments in my career. Seeing my work grace the covers of magazines is wonderful. But nothing compares to getting mail from fans—people who have followed my work for years."

MAKING IT HAPPEN

"I try to operate my business according to three important principles: Always give 110 percent. Always be on time. And always make your client feel appreciated. People starting their own businesses should not expect instant gratification. If you have a passion and you're willing to work hard, the money will come."

PAMELA BUNDY

Like her mother and grandmother, Pamela D. Bundy picked tomatoes while growing up on the family farm in Hustle, Virginia. But her dream was to become a businesswoman. So in 1984, after graduating from Lincoln University in Pennsylvania, she pursued a management career at Southland Corporation's 7-Eleven. Four years later Bundy was laid off and forced to reevaluate her career. She decided to go into business for herself, despite the uncertainty and gripping fear. Using the $17,000 she had saved while working, Bundy took a real-estate appraisal course and successfully launched her company, which became Bundy Development Corporation, primarily developing single-family houses. Today she runs her company with eight employees and is a partner on two large contracts in Washington, D.C.—a $700 million convention center redevelopment project and a $250 million wax museum.

LAYING THE FOUNDATION

"When I got fired, I cried like a baby, but I knew instinctively that I would never work for anyone again. As I had always been interested in real estate, I used my savings as seed money to start my new career. Once I decided to start my own company, I had to cut my personal expenses to the bare bone. So I moved out of my apartment and into my grandmother's house. I began working from a couch in my bedroom. I didn't move out of my grandmother's apartment and buy my own six-bedroom home—which I purchased in a foreclosure deal—until I was completely sure my development company would thrive."

BUILDING FROM SCRATCH

"Every real-estate development deal is different. There is absolutely no floor plan nor can you follow a recipe. For each deal, the financing is different, and so is the team. That is what makes it so fascinating. There are many risks involved in this process: I am sitting with a piece of land and I have to pay a mortgage and an entire team through predevelopment—the engineer, the architect, the legal team."

DEVELOPING REAL ESTATE

"Initially I was flipping houses—I would move in, renovate the house, then sell it for a profit. Because I was savvy with savings, in a decade I was able to accumulate $400,000. That was in 1999. I needed that money to take my business to the next level—developing upscale residential and commercial properties. For my first big deal—five houses in downtown Washington, D.C.—I went to the bank with the $400,000 and obtained the $1.2 million in financing I needed for that project. It put me in the league with established developers."

MAKING IT HAPPEN

"I've never been afraid to ask questions. I've gone out and found mentors, and I listen to them. I sought out development specialists and financial advisers. My success is due to my being a good student."

SIMBA SANA AND YAO AHOTO

Although many small bookstores are being replaced by superstores, Karibu Books is thriving. The company, which started in 1992 as a street-vending operation selling incense, oils and Afrocentric products, now has stores in four Prince George's County, Maryland, malls and a ministore in Arlington, Virginia. Revenues have increased sevenfold since 1995. Karibu co-owners, Simba Sana, 36, a former auditor for Ernst and Young, and his 34-year-old partner, bookseller Yao Ahoto, came together with a commitment to help educate and empower the Black community. Through the written word, their success is a shining example of entrepreneurship at work.

THE TURNING POINT

Sana: "I was working late one night at Ernst and Young and listening to John Coltrane. I remember thinking, I can't see myself doing this for 30 years. I've always had an interest in business, and I had a desire to develop an independent Black institution. On that night, my path became clear."

Ahoto: "My turning point was when my daughter was born. I wanted to create an independent stream of revenue for my child."

GETTING STARTED

Ahoto: "My wife, Karla, and I had decided that there wasn't much to be handed down to our daughter. We invested the money we had saved from working; we had very little to lose. We acquired a vendor license and started selling books."

Sana: "My friend Yao invited me to his book-vending stand near Howard University's campus. I helped him sell on the day after Thanksgiving and we made $417 in four hours. As an accountant, I automatically started calculating how much money I could make if I sold books full-time. I thought I could make as much money as I did at Ernst and Young, but I was way off, and I took a $20,000 hit in salary when I switched careers. Still, I was able to weather that storm."

THE CUSTOMER IS ALWAYS RIGHT

Sana: "We thought that the passion we had for certain types of literature would make our business successful. But if you want to survive in business, you can't just sell what you like."

Ahoto: "While other major bookstores carry some literature that we do, we provide access to core literature targeted toward the legacy and history of our people. It's not guaranteed that someone besides us will do this for our community."

COMMUNITY SERVICE

Sana: "A good bookstore will not only inform our people but will also serve as a haven for Black folks to gather and express themselves."

MAKING IT HAPPEN

Sana: "Creating a solid operation, along with a great location, product and service, is the way to building a good business."

Ahoto: "Take things one day at a time. Be focused on what is in front of you. The journey of a thousand miles begins with a single step."

WATOTO Children's Corner

Left to right:
Yao Ahoto, Simba Sana

YVETTE PETTIT

Upon leaving her native Zimbabwe for the United States, Yvette Pettit, then 20, chose Atlanta as her destination. Starting with an internship at Doppler Studios, a company that produces music, commercial and film projects, Pettit learned every aspect of the business from the ground level, often fetching coffee and running errands. After three years, Pettit, who married a music producer, decided it was time to start her own production company. At age 23 she founded Soapbox Studios by securing a $180,000 refinancing mortgage on their home. Today Soapbox employs eight engineers and editors, and a 10,000-square-foot postproduction facility houses four audio suites and two video suites. Pettit, now 31, has an annual revenue of $2.5 million, and her clients include Nickelodeon Networks and Turner Broadcasting.

RUNNING THE SHOP

"I have had some of the same employees since my company's inception, and we maintain a family-like atmosphere in the workplace—they take care of me and I take care of them. If you treat your employees well, they will be loyal."

RISING TO THE CHALLENGE

"Soapbox Studios competes with larger East Coast companies by meeting a client's needs for half the price of our competitors. I offer my largest clients, such as Turner Broadcasting, very competitive rates for my services. It's rewarding to see several of our promo spots run on television and to have won more than a dozen industry awards for our broadcasts, design and animation."

LESSONS LEARNED

"When I first started my business, there were people who needed my postproduction studio services to complete their film and television projects. I would do the work for free and never hear from them again. Although I am willing to help people and offer lower rates to those in need, I have made a decision to not be taken advantage of."

EXPANDING HER HORIZONS

"Two years ago, using profits from my business, I bought a partnership, for $30,000, in a high-end unisex hair salon, Salon Nede, in downtown Atlanta. We revamped the salon and have attracted a diverse clientele. I love the idea of continually expanding my business ventures. In the next five years I plan to open a Soapbox Studio in Los Angeles and move into creating film trailers and movie scores."

MAKING IT HAPPEN

"Entrepreneurship is about taking risks. I have always gone by my gut instincts and they have never steered me wrong. If you have doubts about a business decision, don't do it. Be in business because you absolutely love it."

Kearn Crockett Cherry

When 38-year-old Kearn Crockett Cherry returned with her husband, Dennis, from Germany, where he had been stationed for five years in the army, they relocated to Arizona and attended college to become certified occupational therapists. After two failed business ventures, the couple and their three children—Denise, Jasmine and Dannan—moved back to Kearn's hometown, Biloxi, Mississippi, to regroup. This time, Kearn invested $15,000 in personal savings to start a home-care staffing company—PRN HomeCare—to provide nursing assistants and general companions for the elderly. In her case, the third attempt was a hit: PRN quickly flourished, and her husband eventually joined the firm.

STRIKE ONE, STRIKE TWO
"While my husband and I were completing classes for our associate degrees, I opened a multicultural gift shop, but I didn't have time to do any marketing or promotion. The store wasn't situated in a heavily traveled location, so my business died. After we received our certification, we started a business that staffed physical therapists. During that time, however, the government enforced budget cutbacks for health-care professionals, and my business crashed. Thanks to the experience of operating two businesses, I was much better prepared the third time around."

STARTING AGAIN
"Although I lost $25,000 in my previous businesses, I wasn't deterred. Marketing and networking are probably the biggest part of the business, so I approached marketing like a zealot. I never lost faith that I could succeed."

KEEPING THE FAITH
"God always provided us with what we needed. One of my clients wanted us to provide a home-care service for her husband. It was then we realized God was telling us it was time to move on."

SEIZING SUCCESS
"Because Americans now are living longer than ever, there is an increasing demand for home-care attendants. Having learned from my past mistakes, I know how crucial proper marketing is to business, so I met with nurses and social workers in more than a dozen hospital centers to spread the word about the service my business could offer their patients."

WORKING AS A TEAM
"My husband and I have been together since 1982, when we were in high school. We have found that two heads are always better than one, and we've complemented each other's strengths. I handle all the administrative tasks and market our services, and he handles staffing, which is the hardest part."

MAKING IT HAPPEN
"The key to any successful business is getting your name and face out there. You must continually market your business. Even if you hire employees to handle marketing campaigns, you must stay involved in the community that you serve."

ANGELA BOONE

For Angela Boone, the choice between wearing heels or hard hats to work is a no-brainer. As owner of Boone International, a full-service construction and engineering design firm in Detroit, this 43-year-old has built her career—quite literally—from the ground up. She has won major state contracts, one for a whopping $275 million, during her seven years in business. A savvy engineer and entrepreneur, Boone is working to tear down stereotypes about Black women in construction—and women in general—one brick at a time.

THE GIFT OF FREEDOM

"When I first started this business in 1997, I had only $700 in savings. I was a single parent and struggling financially. A friend asked me what I wanted for my birthday, and I realized that the best gift I could possibly receive was the opportunity to leave my full-time job as a manufacturing engineer at General Motors. So he bought me an office space with a desk, a fax machine, a file cabinet and three phone lines. I left my job and have never looked back. There were days when the lights, gas and phones got cut off, but since I loved what I was doing, the sacrifices were worth it."

ODD WOMAN OUT

"In the construction business, first you've got to convince people that as a woman you know what you're doing. And then you've got to show them that as a Black person you're good at it. There is a lot of discrimination, and it's a constant struggle. There were times when I've gotten so discouraged that I wanted to give up. But through it all, I get a lot of satisfaction from bucking the odds and working to be one of the best."

LAYING THE FOUNDATION

"I have had a love for design and construction for as long as I can remember. When I was a little girl, I built a big house for my Barbie dolls out of furniture in my mother's house. Construction has always been my passion. That, and my faith in God, is what keeps me going when times get rough."

BUSINESS IS BOOMING

"In 1999 my company was chosen to build a water-treatment plant here in Detroit, and it was our first contract. At $250 million, that was a huge opportunity. I now have 12 employees and I hire independent contractors for each project."

A BRIGHTER TOMORROW

"One way that I stay connected to myself, in addition to all my work, is through community service. One of my biggest goals has always been to open a high-school trade academy. Because I've never been the type of person who enjoyed traditional schooling, I thought it would be helpful to provide technical training to kids who may not want to go to college, but want to learn career-building skills. I hope to open that school in the future."

MAKING IT HAPPEN

"Always be prepared for disappointments when going into business. In the beginning I had some rough times. You have to be prepared, have faith and know that God will handle the rest."

Deborah Tillman

In 1992, when new mother Deborah Tillman could not find quality child care for her son Zepplin, she channeled her concerns into a much-needed and thriving business. Today the 42-year-old Lake Ridge, Virginia, resident owns and runs the Happy Home Child Learning Center, Inc., an early-childhood–education center. Serving children ages 1 to 5, the business has 19 employees and generates more than a half a million dollars annually. With two locations, an infant center on the way and a recently published book, *Stepping Out in Faith: How to Open Up a Quality Childcare Center*, wife, mom and author Tillman has made her passion a reality, a business built on love.

CATALYST FOR CHANGE

"When Zepplin was born, I was working as a staff accountant. My husband and I were looking for someone to care for him, and we researched more than 15 child-care providers. We interviewed, checked references and finally found one after five months. When I came home unexpectedly one day, I found Zepplin in his bassinet, with an empty bottle in his mouth that was propped up by the ledge. I quit my job the next day."

IN THE BEGINNING

"I started out as a home-care provider because I didn't trust anyone with my child. I took a 25-hour course to become licensed, and I interviewed parents to make sure we were a good match. I ran the business out of my apartment for six months. All the while, I was thinking bigger, that I would open a center."

DREAMS COME TRUE

"I started inquiring about available space from a property manager of an apartment complex. After hearing about my good work, the property manager called me in 1993 and offered me a 5,600-square-foot center, which was a previous child-care center that had been closed down.

My husband and I used $7,000 in savings to renovate the center. We officially opened in March 1994. I took out a bank loan to open its sister school in 1998."

FOLLOW YOUR HEART

"I had a bachelor's degree before Zepplin was born, and I earned a master's degree in 2002. I worked from 9:00 A.M. to 6:00 P.M., then went to night school while my husband took care of our son. I was motivated and could not be turned around. God doesn't give us the spirit of fear when He shows us our purpose."

ELEMENTS OF SUCCESS

"Persistence and dedication keep me going. I saw a goal, and I wasn't going to let anything get in my way. My major task was to learn how to delegate, so I hired good people who could make use of their gifts and talents. I always tell the children that the sky is the limit."

MAKING IT HAPPEN

"Learn to delegate. Never compromise your morals, values and goals for anything. Always keep God first."

BUILDING HOME-EQUITY WEALTH

So you want to buy a home, but you're nervous about financing your dream. Whether you are a first-time home buyer, want a more expensive home or are looking for investment property, relax! The process of getting a mortgage has become less time-consuming and intimidating. Lenders can now process a mortgage application faster by checking your credit score. Get started now.

CLEAN UP YOUR CREDIT REPORT. A credit report paints a picture of your account-payment history. A good way to keep your credit score high is to pay your bills on time, avoid using your credit cards past 80 percent of their limits and avoid applying for too many cards. Before mortgage shopping, order your report from the three major credit-reporting agencies and correct any errors. Incorrect negative information can inflate your interest rate or disqualify you. A previous bankruptcy may not prevent you from getting a mortgage—if you now pay bills on time and if you've had a clean payment history since the bankruptcy was discharged—but your interest rate may be higher. Get a copy of your credit report from Experian, (888) 397-3742; Equifax, (800) 685-1111; and TransUnion, (800) 888-4213. Follow the instructions on the reports, and to dispute any inaccuracies, make sure all information is up to date.

DON'T BUY MORE THAN YOU CAN AFFORD. Determine what you can comfortably pay each month for housing. Keep in mind that in addition to principal and interest, you'll have to pay real-estate taxes and insurance. You'll also need funds for maintenance and repairs. Before extending a loan, lenders generally look at your debt-to-income ratio—debt payments (excluding rent) divided by gross monthly income (before deductions). For instance, if you make $3,000 a month and pay $600 toward your debt, your ratio is 20 percent ($600 ÷ $3,000 = 0.20), which is considered good. A higher ratio suggests a need to control spending. Lenders view you favorably when your monthly mortgage payment equals no more than about 29 percent of your monthly gross income.

SHOP FOR THE BEST MORTGAGE. Get interest-rate quotes from at least three lending institutions or brokers before settling on one. Get referrals from your realtor, friends and family members who have recently purchased homes, or check the local Yellow Pages, newspapers or Internet search engines. A fraction of a percent difference in an interest rate can save you thousands of dollars over the life of the loan, so shop around. Your first choice doesn't have to be a 30-year fixed-rate mortgage, especially if you plan to stay in the home for less than seven years. Compare interest rates to see if an adjustable rate mortgage (ARM) is a better financial fit. If you can afford a higher monthly payment, consider a 15- or 20-year mortgage that may have a lower rate, thus saving you money in the long run.

PROTECT YOURSELF FROM PREDATORY LENDING PRACTICES. These might include steering customers toward higher interest rates, assessing unnecessary fees or adding points without reducing the interest rate. If you suspect you're a target, ask an official at a nonprofit housing agency or legal-aid organization to review the proposed offer and advise you if it's sound.

NEGOTIATE CLOSING COSTS. You should receive a Good Faith Estimate of Closing Costs when you apply for a loan. This gives you an idea of the lender's charges for origination and discount fees, credit report, appraisal, title insurance, document preparation, termite inspection and other costs, and it tells you how much out-of-pocket money you'll need to pay. Request an itemization of closing costs from each lender before submitting an application. Inquire about charges on one lender's list that are not on others'; this may prevent undisclosed fees from surprising you at settlement. Select a lender who is willing to answer your questions and help you navigate the mortgage terrain. Expect the officer to ask questions. Your replies can give her important cues about the best

mortgage program to suggest. Sellers are often willing to help with closing costs, so negotiate.

GET YOUR OWN EXPERTS. Get a lawyer to review the purchase contract and make sure your interests are protected. You'll also save a bundle in unforeseen repairs if you hire a house inspector who is very reputable in the business and who may uncover hidden problems like termites or structural defects before you seal the deal. Also understand that the real-estate agent works for the seller— unless you have a "buyer agency agreement." Without one, if you tell the agent, "I just love this place, and I'd pay the $130,000 asking price, but I'll offer $110,000," the agent is obligated to tell the seller you're willing to pay more.

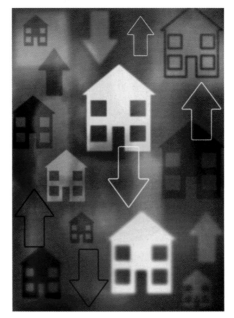

23 Real-Estate Terms You Should Know

Buying a home may be one of the largest investments you'll make in a lifetime. So enhance your real-estate savvy by getting acquainted with these terms before you begin your search.

ADJUSTABLE-RATE MORTGAGE (ARM): A loan with an interest rate that fluctuates periodically according to prevailing interest rates in the markets. Because borrowers take on some of the risk of rates rising, they will receive a lower initial rate than they would get on a fixed-rate mortgage.

AMORTIZATION: The gradual elimination of a liability, such as a mortgage, by regular payments of the principal and interest over a period of time. A percentage of each payment goes toward interest, while the remainder reduces the principal.

APPRAISAL: Evaluation of an asset, such as a home, to determine its value. For home owners, this may be based on comparable sales and/or the ability of the property to build income.

BALLOON MORTGAGE: A short-term mortgage in which the borrower makes small periodic payments until the term is completed, with a final lump-sum payment.

CLOSING COSTS: Settlement costs paid by a seller and buyer when the purchase is finalized. This amount may include fees for appraisals, credit reports, mortgage insurance, title-insurance premium, property taxes and attorney costs.

CONDOMINIUM: A form of property ownership that has individually owned units in a multiunit building, with shared ownership of common areas.

CONSTRUCTION LOAN: A short-term loan to finance building a real-estate project, such as a new home. The funds are disbursed to the borrower as needed and repaid after the project is completed.

CONVERTIBLE ARM: An adjustable-rate mortgage that allows borrowers to switch to a fixed-rate mortgage under specific conditions.

CO-OP: A multiunit housing complex where residents own shares in the corporation that possesses the property.

EQUITY: The difference between what you owe on your home and the current fair market value.

ESCROW: Money deposited at closing with a third party—usually to pay taxes and insurance—until all terms of the agreement are satisfied.

FAIR MARKET VALUE: The amount at which the buyer and the seller agree to complete a transaction, based on comparable selling prices of area properties.

FIXED-RATE MORTGAGE: A loan with an interest rate that is constant throughout the life of the mortgage. Because the rate doesn't fluctuate with changes in market conditions, it is normally higher than variable rates.

LIEN: A claim against a property for payment of debt, either voluntary or involuntary.

MORTGAGE: A legal agreement that pledges a property to a lender as security for payment on a loan that can span as many as 30 years.

MORTGAGE BROKER: An intermediary between a lender and borrower who helps the buyer find a loan. Once the terms have been set, the broker doesn't help finance the mortgage.

POINTS: Charges assessed by the lender that are added to the amount of the mortgage and payable at closing. One point equals 1 percent of the face value of the loan.

PREQUALIFICATION: The process of determining the eligibility of the buyer for approval of a mortgage, based on the borrower's credit history and income.

PRINCIPAL: Amount financed and due to lender, excluding interest, insurance and taxes.

PRIVATE MORTGAGE INSURANCE (PMI): Insurance to protect the lender against losses owing to default or foreclosure. Borrowers are required to have PMI on a conventional loan that has a down payment of less than 20 percent.

REFINANCING: The process of paying off one loan with the proceeds from a new loan using the same property as security.

SECOND MORTGAGE: A loan that uses the equity in your home as security.

TITLE INSURANCE: A policy that insures purchasers against title-search errors. Insurance to protect a lender or owner against loss in the event of a property ownership dispute. The policy protects only the title defects that exist at the time of title transfer.

5 WAYS TO RAISE YOUR CREDIT SCORE

When it comes to financing anything, your credit score is everything. Getting a thumbs-up or -down depends on your score—a credit-rating system developed by Fair Isaac Corp. that tells lenders how likely you are to pay your bills on time. Credit scores from FICO range from 300 to 850, with the average score around 750. A score of 700 or above is considered healthy; a score below 620 could mean that you'll be denied a mortgage or that you'll have to pay a higher interest rate. Here are some tips from myfico.com to help you raise your score.

1. *Pay all bills on time.* Late payments are recorded on your credit report and can lower your score. If you've missed payments, catch up. The better your bill-paying habits, the higher your score.

2. *Keep balances low.* High outstanding debt on credit cards and other revolving credit can decrease your score.

3. *Don't apply for credit too often.* Every time you apply for credit, an inquiry is placed in your file. Too many new credit applications can lower your score.

4. *Don't close unused credit cards.* This strategy will not raise your score. But don't open new credit-card accounts that you don't need—just in order to increase your available credit. This approach could actually lower your score.

5. *Don't have too few credit accounts.* If you have no loans or credit accounts, you are also considered a credit risk. A few credit cards in good standing, with reasonable limits and balances, can help improve your score.

If denied credit, log on to www.ftc.gov/bcp/conline/pubs/credit/crdright.htm to learn about your rights under the Equal Opportunity Act.

You are the brand

"**I** treat this as art but also as a business, and I have from day one. I've built a brand."

—TYLER PERRY

TYLER PERRY

Tyler Perry began writing to deal with his difficult childhood, and he still bears the scars of a teenage suicide attempt. Now, with seven productions grossing more than $60 million over the last few years, Perry has become America's most accomplished young playwright. His plays, which include *Medea's Class Reunion* and *I Can Do Bad All By Myself*, have contributed to the rebirth of urban theater nationwide. However, he is far from being an overnight success. Perry found the road to success paved with challenges. After moving from his native New Orleans to Atlanta, he spent years in odd jobs and at times was homeless and hopeless. Writing saved his life and was his ticket to success. He is held in such high regard that evangelist T.D. Jakes tapped him to assist in the production of *Woman, Thou Art Loosed!*

ESCAPE TO DESTINY

"As a child, I never heard 'I love you' from my father. I never got a hug. Instead of 'How was school today?' I would be greeted with a backhand because I was writing or drawing. That was too soft for a son of his. But the terrible moments had a purpose. I withdrew, went inside myself to create a world of escape, and little did I know that I was carving out my destiny."

HARD KNOCKS

"I saved $12,000—from working as a used-car salesman and bill collector and in hotel housekeeping, where I shined shoes—before I could rent a very small theater in Atlanta. It was a 200-seat theater, and I put on *I Know I've Been Changed*, which was my first show. Over the course of a weekend I expected 800 people to attend, but only 30 people came and I lost everything. I had the rent money, the car note, everything tied up in the production. This would happen again and again to me over six years."

GOD'S VOICE

"I knew that God was telling me to do this. I would leave my jobs because they wouldn't give me the time off to travel and rehearse. I stepped out on faith, believing that it would be okay."

TURNING POINT

"It was the coldest night in Atlanta ever, March 12, 1998. The heat goes out in the building, and I'm sitting in the dressing room freezing. I tell God, 'I'm not doing this anymore!' and He says, 'I am God: You don't tell Me when it's over.' Then He tells me to look out the window. There is a line of theatergoers around the corner. It was amazing. We sold out eight shows. When it hit, it hit."

PLAYWRITING PHILOSOPHY

"I keep it simple. Forgiveness is a powerful thing. And in every show I do, there's always that underlying theme: Forgive and move on."

MAKING IT HAPPEN

"I treat this as art but also as a business, and I have from day one. I've built a brand. When people see the name Tyler Perry, they know they'll laugh all the way through a show, but they'll also leave with something they can use in life."

TYRA BANKS

Given the fact that both her parents were successful business executives, it's not surprising that Tyra Banks had her heart set on becoming a film and television executive herself. After she completed high school, an Elite Model Agency scout spotted the five-foot ten-inch beauty, and she went off to Paris in 1991, garnering immediate success on the catwalk. Returning to these shores, Banks made fashion breakthroughs: In 1994 she became the first Black model to grace the cover of the *Sports Illustrated* swimsuit edition and was named one of *People* magazine's 50 Most Beautiful People. She landed several lucrative contracts, including Cover Girl cosmetics and Victoria's Secret and snagged several television roles. In 2003 the bankable beauty finally made her producing dreams come true by creating the highly rated reality-show series *America's Next Top Model*.

SUPERMODEL SAVES THE DAY

"When I came up with *America's Next Top Model*, I didn't want to just sell my idea to a network, I wanted to be the executive producer and involved in every aspect of the show. I worked out a deal with UPN-TV. Now the show is the highest-rated program they've ever had in that time slot. The series provides opportunities for girls who might not get the big break that I did in modeling. It takes more than looks: It takes confidence, energy and brains. I don't take it easy on the girls because I have to train them for the dog-eat-dog world they so want to be a part of."

SAVING WITH INTEREST

"I have always been cheap. When I was younger, my mother gave me a monthly allowance because she knew I wouldn't spend it all right away. Since the beginning of my modeling career, I've been saving money and investing it. I never indulged in items such as flashy cars, jewelry and clothes or wasted money on lavish entertainment."

BANKING ON YOUR YOUTH

"I loved camp as a kid. Girl Scouts camp was the first place that exposed me to other cultures and types of girls. I loved the idea that you met these girls and by the end of the week you had built a sisterhood. I wanted girls I'd met to meet other girls like them. So my camp Tzone was born—a free weeklong camp where teenage girls build independence and enhance self-esteem. Modeling and the show are my income, but Tzone is my heart. Now I want to hold camps in cities across the country."

MAKING IT HAPPEN

"I want to be in charge of myself, in control of my career and to be more of a businesswoman. I wanted to take this name I had made for myself and take it to other mediums and levels—and that is what I continue to do. You can be a businesswoman and a producer long after the boobs have fallen and the looks have faded. And that is what real power is all about."

EVE

Eve Jihan Jeffers—better known simply as Eve—went through growing pains in high school and had lost her way as a teenager. She wandered into dangerous territory looking for the love absent in her life. She wasn't focused and spent her time pursuing the rap game, which she started professionally right out of high school. But the hits didn't start coming until 1999, after she left Dr. Dre's label and signed with the Yonkers-based Ruff Ryders hip-hop label. After the self-proclaimed "pit bull in a skirt" successfully conquered rap, she decided to branch out. In 2002 Eve made her acting debut in the hit film *Barbershop,* and the positive reviews she received resulted in her own self-titled television show. In 2003 the rapper–actress added clothing designer to her list of achievements. Eve's clothing line, Fetish, mixes high style with urban glamour. The line resembles the lady herself.

SCHOOL DAZE

"I got in trouble for cutting school, staying out late, lying about detention and lying about homework. I hated high school. I got punished a lot. I lost my way, but deep inside I always knew there was something else, many good things I could do."

PAYING DUES

"I worked as a stripper for only a little while, but it helped me realize that this was not where I was supposed to be. This was not my life. I did it because I was trying to be grown up. That was my rebellion. I was out of high school, and I needed money. That was it. I just pray to God I never have to go back to that. Ever."

CURRENT PROSPECTS

"Right now I love where I am. I feel free, and I've moved into other areas I love, like film and clothing design."

WHY CLOTHING?

"I figured, why not? I got tired of asking designers for clothes; it was time to start wearing my own stuff. I hope to be one of the first young Black female designers to introduce a line that truly reflects our sense of style. Overall, I want my clothes to scream, 'I'm comfortable with who I am!' "

THE FLAVA OF FETISH

"It's a fun line—kinda like urban couture. The line is definitely feminine and sophisticated, but I want women to feel empowered, sexy and independent when they wear Fetish. A woman should dress from the inside out, and she should always wear what she feels most comfortable in. Black women are creative dressers. We take the traditional and the trendy and give it our own flavor."

MAKING IT HAPPEN

"I love to see us continually evolving and changing. And that's what keeps things exciting."

OPRAH WINFREY

Oprah's an icon, and she's everywoman. She has it all, and she's triumphed over adversity. We know her well: host of the nation's top-rated talk show, Oscar-nominated actress, winner of numerous Emmy awards, film producer, philanthropist. And she's the richest Black woman on the planet. Our first Black woman billionaire launched *O, The Oprah Magazine*, and she runs the Live Your Best Life Tour, a seminar that helps people find their true calling in life. Her generosity has brought hope and love to so many—and helping impoverished African children has become her life's mission. We cherish and revere her for all she is and all she does. She's for real.

ON THE OPRAH MAGAZINE

"When I first started the magazine, people were always saying, 'Well, who else are you going to put on the cover?' And I'd say, 'Well, who's going to sell better than I am? You got any ideas?' I wouldn't say I take it in stride, though, because sometimes I'm in awe of it myself. I'll see myself on my own magazine cover, and I go, 'That's me.' "

BEING HERSELF

"I understand why I would be a puzzlement. I don't play sports, I don't sing, I don't look like your typical movie star. I think for a culture of people who have been for so many years denied and deprived and lacking in self-esteem, it's very hard to see the possibility of what awaits in your future. It's really hard because the world has given you ideas about who you can be. It takes a lot of courage to be who you really are and not let the rest of the world tell you what that is."

GIVING TO SOUTH AFRICAN CHILDREN

"I plan to build a dozen schools on the continent, the first one being a leadership academy for girls. Women are going to save Africa. And this will be my legacy. All around Africa you will have these women coming out of these schools with a future so bright it burns their eyes—that's what Quincy Jones once said about my future. I realized this is why I was born. These are my children. This is why I don't have any children. This is why I never married."

MAKING IT HAPPEN

"I feel tremendously powerful because I do believe I have reached a point in life where my personality is aligned with what my soul came to do. I believe you have to use your ego for a higher good."

BEYONCÉ

Girl groups have been the launching pad for some of the music industry's most successful artists: Diana Ross had her Supremes, Patti LaBelle had her Bluebells—and Beyoncé Giselle Knowles has Destiny's Child. With a string of hits—from "Independent Woman" in 1999 to "Survivor" in 2001—Destiny's Child quickly became a top-ten mainstay. In that same year, Beyoncé took the group's strong-Black-woman lyrics to another level and embarked on solo projects. Her career trajectory has been rising ever since. Soon after her starring role in the television movie *Carmen* and her big-screen debut in the *Austin Powers* sequel, *Goldmember,* she received offers from Pepsi and L'Oréal for endorsement contracts. Then her first solo CD, *Dangerously in Love,* debuted in 2003 and went multiplatinum. Now, along with her mother, Tina, the Houston native is launching a clothing line, A Touch of Couture, and she has collaborated with Tommy Hilfiger Toiletries to develop a perfume line. And this multitalented minimogul is only 23 years old.

LEAVING HOME

"My job has forced me to mature fast, especially when I did Carmen at 18. I was away from home, and I had to learn a new job and make friends in a new city. I call it my college. Also, looking back to when I had to write the song 'Survivor,' I sometimes think, *How did I do that?* I had to depend on myself, and I had to grow. After that, I felt like I could accomplish anything."

TAKING CARE OF BUSINESS

"I absolutely check my money. I get my statements every week and my mother helps me review them. My money is invested in property. I'm trying to set myself up so that in a couple of years, if I decide to settle down and have a family, I can."

GROWING PAINS

"I've always been involved in the songwriting, the clothes I wear and my videos. Now I'm involved with deciding everything—from which magazines I appear in to my schedule. I recently moved to Miami, away from everything in my comfort zone, and started working with producers by myself. I've matured tremendously over the past three years. I'm proud of the fact that I trusted my instincts and everything worked out."

MAKING IT HAPPEN

"As long as the quality of the work is there and as long as I keep being picky about the things that I do, I'll be fine."

JANET JACKSON

With patience and poise, she climbed to the heights of superstardom, proving that she is a woman in control. From her childhood into her teens, Janet Jackson made a name for herself through her acting, in such television shows as *Good Times, Diff'rent Strokes* and *Fame*. In her twenties, the Jackson singing gene kicked in, and like her famous older brothers, Janet made the musical world sit up and take notice. Beginning with the 1986 release of *Control* and for the next 17 years, Janet has marked her territory, selling more than 50 million albums worldwide and performing to sold-out arenas. She has won a legion of fans who have come to love her for sharing her soul through her music with great honesty.

DECLARATION OF INDEPENDENCE
"To me, growth is everything. As an artist, an entertainer and a Black woman, I'm interested in making strides, taking chances and finding my own way in my own time. I have crafted my art according to my heart. I feel free, and there's nothing more wonderful than freedom."

FAME'S PAYOFF
"The best thing about being famous is being able to help people and to know that I've helped change someone's life. After *Rhythm Nation* was released, I heard from kids who said that they had contemplated suicide, but after listening to this album, their lives completely turned in another direction. I've always said that I feel I was put on this earth to help people. And if it's through music, so be it."

MONEY MATTERS
"It's very important to invest and to watch your money. I'm not into letting other people sign things for me. Granted, there are times when you have to, but giving all that power to one person is just asking for trouble. I hired someone to watch the books, and I have monthly meetings to keep on top of how everything is going."

MAKING IT HAPPEN
"I used to think work meant only physical tasks, but now I realize that the work ethic applies to the spiritual as well. Discovering who you are, independent of anyone or anything, is perhaps the hardest work of all. That's the work that interests me the most—the work that, with God's help, can bring a deeper sense of satisfaction."

VENUS WILLIAMS

When Venus Williams first flashed across our television screens, braids and beads swinging, we knew the sport of professional tennis would never be the same—for us, anyway. Critics scoffed at her look, her training and her style, but millions of us cheered proudly for the little girl from Compton, California, who took the tennis world by storm. By now, most know the stats: She played her first tournament at 4 years old, was unbeaten in 63 games by age 10, became a pro at 14, is a winner of the Grand Slams—French Open, Wimbledon, U.S. Open, Australian Open—and won an Olympic gold medal, all before her twenty-third birthday. Endorsement deals with Avon, McDonalds, Wrigley's/Doublemint Gum, Wilson's Racquet Sports and Nortel Networks soon followed, and a $40 million endorsement deal with Reebok was the largest contract ever awarded to a female athlete. Now Williams is entering another arena—the business world.

EXPLORING NEW TERRITORY

"Tennis doesn't define me. My parents taught me to be well-rounded and more than just an athlete. I've been fortunate, but I've also worked hard. Thankfully, opportunities have come my way, and I'm now able to do other things besides play tennis."

GOING FOR IT

"In my late teens I realized that design was something I wanted to pursue. After decorating my home and enjoying it, I launched V Starr Interiors, a residential interior design and decorating firm located in Palm Beach Gardens, Florida. V Starr, which is my first initial and middle name, is a business that my staff runs daily and I can work on more fully when I'm not on the road. I became a certified interior decorator, and I'm at work to complete a bachelor's degree in the field."

THE NAME IS THE GAME

"Reebok offered me an opportunity to codesign a signature line of apparel and footwear. Wilson's Leather also invited me to create the Venus Williams Collection of leatherwear."

BANKING ON THE FUTURE

"I realize it takes a few years to achieve goals. What's important is that I have goals and I'm reaching them. Eventually, V Starr will grow to include home furnishings and accessories. For now, I have a great staff that works hard and believes in the company."

MONEY MATTERS

"I try to save as much as I can. I'm a girl, so I like clothes, but I don't buy tons of fast, expensive cars. I'm not a lender either. I work hard and don't have any big expenses."

MAKING IT HAPPEN

"Becoming a businesswoman is kind of like playing tennis—you have to keep reinventing yourself and getting better in order to bring something new to the market. For me, it's about longevity, finding projects I truly enjoy, and dedicating myself to them."

SHAPE UP FINANCIALLY!

Sixty percent of Americans are living from paycheck to paycheck, but you can write a different script for yourself. Even if you have no savings and are totally dependent on the next paycheck to meet living expenses, with a new mind-set and a bit of discipline you can be on your way to securing your financial future.

When it comes to expenses, little things, like daily snacks and manicures, add up to a lot. The idea here is to help us see that we shouldn't be working for money—money should work for us.

When was the last time you calculated the amount you spend daily for drinks, food and snacks? These alone can eat up more than $200 a month. If you put that $200 toward an individual retirement account (IRA)—as part of an investment of just $3,000 for the year—an account that earns 8 percent annually may be worth more than $300,000 in 30 years.

But what if you don't splurge on little things but on "keeping up with the Joneses"—maxing out credit cards on clothes and deluxe dinners, burrowing deeper in order to maintain a lifestyle your paycheck can't cover. You can jump off the paycheck-to-paycheck treadmill with these nine simple strategies.

9 STEPS TO FINANCIAL FITNESS

1. TRACK DAILY EXPENDITURES. Keep a detailed list of every penny you spend for a month or two, from packs of gum to movie tickets to lottery tickets to lunch. Jot it all down in a notebook. At the end of the month, examine your spending and determine how much was needless and where you can cut back to create surplus.

2. DEVELOP A SPENDING PLAN. Regardless of how much you earn, take account of what's actually coming in and what's going out. Until you have a plan, you'll be walking around in the dark. Commit to a monthly spending plan or budget. Start by categorizing your expenses and noting how

much of each paycheck is needed to cover each category. You can use a notebook, a ledger, a work sheet, a BudgetMap checkbook register (budgetmap.com) or a computer software program such as Quicken or Microsoft Money. Aim each month to end up with a budget surplus—money saved rather than spent. Reevaluate your budget quarterly and make adjustments as needed.

3. WATCH YOUR APR.

When was the last time you calculated the amount you pay each month to finance credit-card debt? Even when an item is on sale, if you charge it and carry a balance, you can end up paying up to four times as much for it. Let's say you have three cards, each with a $3,000 balance at a 15-percent annual percentage rate (APR). In paying just the interest alone, at the end of a year you'll have shelled out $1,350, and, in five years, $6,750, at the rate of about $112 a month.

4. SLASH CREDIT-CARD DEBT.

If you're paying the minimum on credit-card debt, it can take you almost forever to reach a zero balance. For example, if you owe $2,000 on a card with an 18-percent APR, it will take you 30 years to pay off that amount if you pay only the minimum amount due. One quicker way to get rid of credit-card debt is to target the card with the highest APR and pay more on it each month while paying less on the others. Another strategy is to pay off

the card with the smallest balance first, then pay the card with the next smallest balance, and so on. Each time you pay off one debt, take the amount you had allotted for that payment and put it toward the next targeted bill. But keep in mind that any method you choose will work only if you avoid running up more debt. And if your credit card has an APR higher than 12 percent, consider applying for a card that charges a low- or zero-interest rate, and transfer your balances to it. Check with various banks to find out who gives the lowest rates. Be sure to find out how long the low rate is effective. For information on finding a good deal, check out bankrate.com or cardweb.com.

SAVE BIG BUCKS ON BILLS

You can save thousands of dollars in interest by paying a few dollars more on your credit-card bills each month. Let's say you owe $2,500 at a rate of 15 percent. Instead of shelling out just the minimum amount due, try paying $3 extra each month. You will save $881 in interest, and finish paying the debt seven years sooner. The chart below shows that if you:

Add this amount	You'll save
$3	$881
$25	$2,559
$50	$2,983
$100	$3,261

5. SET FINANCIAL GOALS.

Decide on short- and long-term goals, and develop an action plan to make them happen. Let's say you want to pay off all your credit-card debt or contribute more to your 401(k) or retire at age 57. Make your goals specific and measurable, such as: I want to save $75 more each month ($2.50 every day). Then determine what specific steps you'll take to reach your financial goal—for example, bringing your lunch from home at least four days a week or buying regular coffee instead of the pricey brews. Make sure you write your goals down and review them regularly.

6. LIVE BELOW YOUR MEANS.

Ask yourself: What can I live without? Do I really need to spend $75 or more a month for a deluxe cable plan? Or spend hundreds on cell-phone chitchat? Or pay $500 for a designer handbag? Living below your means requires spending on what you need, not on what you want or what your girlfriend has. You can do it if you change some of your behavior, such as eating fewer dinners out, brown-bagging it or renting movies occasionally instead of going to the theater. And stop charging: Pay with cash or use a debit card. If your take-home pay is $30,000 a year, try spending as if it's $25,000. You can use the other $5,000 to invest more in your 401(k) or another investment plan, pay off debt, create an emergency fund or make a down payment on a home or investment property. You'll build a sizable nest egg by just taking a few steps to cut spending.

7. PAY YOURSELF FIRST.

Before you pay your rent, mortgage, bills or car loan, have at least 10 percent of your paycheck automatically deducted to go into a savings account, your 401(k) or an individual retirement account (IRA). This will discipline you. And it guarantees that money is saved and invested to secure your financial future.

8. INCREASE WITHHOLDING ALLOWANCES.

If you typically get a fat tax-refund check, one way to get more in your paycheck is to increase your tax-withholding allowances on Form W-4. Each allowance reduces the amount of tax that's withheld from your paycheck. So instead of giving Uncle Sam an interest-free loan, use that money to invest, pay off debt or build up an emergency fund.

9. GROW YOUR INCOME.

There are a host of things you can do to supplement your earnings. Turn a hobby into a gig on the side, find a direct-sales company that sells products you love— Avon, Warm Spirit, Mary Kay. Find a higher-paying job or part-time work, and earmark the additional money for paying down debts. If your debt is overwhelming, ask your creditors to lower the interest rate or the minimum amount due. For credit-counseling or debt-reduction services, contact the nonprofit National Foundation for Credit Counseling at nfcc.org or debtadvice.org, or call (800) 388-2227.

5 Ways to Live as if You're Rich

Not exactly rolling with the nouveau riche clique? Try modeling yourself on the old-money rich, who are notable for the squeeze they put on a dollar. Here are five frugal ways to emulate them without ending up in the poorhouse.

1. Buy pre-owned prestige.
If you must have a BMW, Cadillac, Mercedes or Lexus, buy a used one. Businesses lease a large number of luxury cars for their employees, and many of these vehicles are not purchased at the end of the lease agreements. These previously driven prestige cars usually have low mileage and are in good condition.

2. Shop for the deal.
Something low-priced isn't necessarily a good deal, especially if it ends up hanging unworn in your closet. Buy for quality, style and service at outlets, resale shops and men's stores, where unisex items—sweaters, T-shirts—usually cost less.

3. Travel on the cheap.
Opportunities abound for globe-trotting on a shoestring. Do research: Airfares fluctuate by hundreds of dollars. There are several discount travel sites to log on to—type in "cheap travel" into a search engine.

4. Polish your taste within a spending limit.
Throw out the fake flowers and plastic dishes; then set a spending limit on replacements. Rummage through antique shops and thrift stores for linen and lace tableware, crystal, silver and china to add old-money charm to your home.

5. Stop charging and switch to debit cards or cash.
But keep track of purchases with the debit card, because it can lull you into spending as if you're really rich.

PASSION INTO PROFIT

"**E**nter a field that you absolutely love, because it will provide a buffer against the setbacks, hardships and sacrifices you will have to make."

—LAVETTA WILLIS

LAVETTA WILLIS

After playing college basketball for Notre Dame, where she earned a B.S. in electrical engineering in 1988, stunning six-footer Lavetta Willis was determined to create her own company in the athletic-apparel arena. With corporate giants like Nike, Adidas and Reebok dominating the market, few people believed in her dream. But Willis was determined and prepared. In 1998 she founded the LL International Shoe Co. in Los Angeles and now has a production facility in China. She's the only Black female president and CEO in the game, and her cutting-edge men's and women's apparel and athletic-footwear business cashes in $60 million annually. Securing endorsements from NBA superstars—such as Chris Webber, Latrell Sprewell and Karl Malone—the 38-year-old Wayne, Michigan, native sells her products in more than 200 retail outlets nationwide.

MANEUVERS FOR THE MISSION
"My professional goal is for kids to believe that my company has the number one athletic shoe on the streets when it comes to innovation and quality. During my basketball days, I was forced to wear apparel and shoes that didn't fit properly. Now I make sure that both female and male customers are getting the best possible products available. And in today's marketplace, sneakers rule."

SETTING UP HER SLAM DUNK
"While I was attending law school, I was introduced to Karl Malone, whose daughter wore a size 14 shoe. He loved my idea of making athletic shoes to fit and introduced me to a factory in China. As a result, I never practiced one day of law. At the same time, I met designer Lantz Simpson and we formed a partnership. We didn't want venture capitalists to fund our operation, so we scraped together money from our family, friends and savings and ate peanut-butter-and-jelly sandwiches. We started collecting orders, and once we had enough, we went to a bank and were able to

secure a factor agreement to provide us with the funds we needed to fill the orders. We shipped our first shoe in the spring of 1998."

FIGHT THE POWER
"I wanted recognition as an athletic brand, so I pursued the necessary technology to achieve my goal. In 2001 we manufactured our first high-performance running shoe, Sole Sonic Force. Retailers loved it, and so did customers. Suddenly we found ourselves in a patent-infringement lawsuit with Nike Corp., who claimed that our athletic shoe was too similar to theirs. It was a frightening and disappointing experience. Eventually we reached a settlement, and my company continues to thrive."

MAKING IT HAPPEN
"Any business in which there is the possibility of large financial gain is extremely competitive. Enter a field that you absolutely love, because it will provide a buffer against the setbacks, hardships and sacrifices you will have to make."

BARBARA EL WILSON

When she was a child, Barbara El Wilson's father nicknamed her Sugarfoot, a term of endearment frequently used by folks in the South. Her mother told her that Sugarfoots were lovable dolls created in a southern village. The joy Barbara felt while playing with her rag dolls remained with her through adulthood, and she began making dolls as a hobby. In 1992, this Washington, D.C.–based entrepreneur turned her hobby into Sugarfoots—a unique line of handmade dolls that have cocoa, ginger and cinnamon complexions and wear colorful pinafores, pantaloons and overalls.

A CUT ABOVE
"These are not like your average rag dolls. They come in the brightest, most vibrant colors. Every culture is represented by the bright colors, and I want the dolls to show that. I want them to have a crossover feel."

MARKETING 101
"Ten years ago, on a visit to West Africa, I saw women carrying their wares in large baskets. Once I got home, I started carrying my dolls everywhere, even on the subway. I used to put the dolls in a big basket and pass out flyers. I sold a lot of dolls that way, but I can remember having calluses on my hands from the basket. Now everything is basically through mail order."

GROWING PAINS
"By 1998 I was taking orders from New York's FAO Schwarz, the California African-American Museum store, the Smithsonian Museum Shop in Washington, D.C., and countless specialty stores in the U.S. Virgin Islands. To keep the dolls on store shelves, I had to relinquish making each doll personally, which takes up to four and a half hours. So now I contract some of the work out."

BUILDING MOMENTUM
"I can feel it picking up steam. Somebody came up to me in Washington's Eastern Market and said, 'Hey, you're the Sugarfoots lady.' I'm starting to get that all the time."

BRANCHING OUT
"In 1999 I created Sugarfoots Theatre Workshop to introduce youngsters to the art of storytelling. And in September 2001, I created the Sugarfoots series of children's books. My dolls make the grumpiest people smile, and for me, that's the best part of all."

MAKING IT HAPPEN
"Find the most creative means possible to get your product out. Face-to-face eye contact with people allowed me to gain exposure for my dolls. No matter how good your product is, if no one knows about it, it's just a great product."

AMY HILLIARD

After 20 years in corporate America, Amy Hilliard, a marketing executive, took a leap of faith. Leaving behind job security and a six-figure salary, she followed her sweet tooth and her heart, and turned her love for pound cakes into a lucrative business. Hilliard, a 51-year-old Detroit native, launched the ComfortCake Company four years ago. Based in Chicago, it now supplies more than 100 stores nationwide and has been featured on the Home Shopping Network. Also, the cakes are sold on amazon.com. The ComfortCake Company is a hit no matter how you slice it.

TAKING A CHANCE
"In 2000 I made a decision to go out on my own after a satisfying career during which I had launched new products for Gillette, Soft Sheen and L'Oréal. I decided I didn't want to look over my life and wish I had done my own thing. After consulting with my family, I sold my home with one goal in mind: to finance my dream of becoming the premium producer of pound cakes. My children work for me part-time in the summer. My son is my chief taste tester, and my 17-year-old daughter has a keen marketing sense. She came up with the slogan 'Pound cake so good it feels like a hug,' and it's on every box. My husband has also been totally supportive."

COOKING UP A PLAN
"For Thanksgiving in 1999, I couldn't cook the turkey because I kept getting requests to make pound cakes. After I'd made about 30 cakes I thought, *I must have something here. If my family can go crazy over my pound cakes, others might, too.* Then at a Christmas party, someone tasted one of my liqueur-infused cakes and said, 'Wow, this is a comfortable cake.' That was it! I decided it was time to follow my passion. I filed for a trademark and Web site domain name (comfortcake.com) and put my dream into action."

NO CAKEWALK
"It was difficult to find a bakery that could fill large orders and bake our cakes from scratch. Through networking we landed a meeting with United Airlines, which led us to our current baker."

LET THEM EAT CAKE
"Two days after we met with United, the airline ordered 500,000 slices to be served on its Hawaii flights. Then came our biggest client, the Chicago public-school system, which has served students more than 2 million slices."

LEAD BY EXAMPLE
"As an entrepreneur you have to be concerned with every aspect of your business. The buck stops with you, and that's a very difficult responsibility if you're not prepared for it. And everybody has to pitch in. I won't ask my staff—three employees and 14 manufacturers—to do anything I wouldn't do. Your employees need to know that they have a leader who is willing to go above and beyond—and then they will, too."

MAKING IT HAPPEN
"Starting a business is tough. Be committed to making it happen; you must have faith. Combine instinct, intellect and integrity, and lead with your heart. And no matter what, stay humble."

TRACY REESE

As a teenager growing up in Detroit, Tracy Reese dabbled in fashion as a hobby. But she never thought her love for sketching and sewing outfits would change her career path from architect to clothing designer. As an architectural student at New York's Parsons School of Design, she attended a summer course in fashion design and soon became convinced that it was not just a pastime. Tracy's father, who always believed in her 100 percent—financially and emotionally—invested in her newfound love and helped give birth to her dream. After an earlier false start, she launched the Tracy Reese line in 1993, specializing in giving vintage ideas a modern spin. Her two collections, Tracy Reese and Plenty—a funky and more casual line—earned $10 million in 2002 and are carried by such top-tier department stores as Neiman Marcus and Saks Fifth Avenue. For more than a decade, Reese's delicate details and tailoring have made her a queen of feminine chic.

STEPPING OUT

"It was my dad's idea that I launch my own line. I had worked for design houses like Arlequin Paris, Perry Ellis and Magaschoni, but when you're working for a company, your ideas become part of a group effort. I needed freedom and choice. Once I got over my fear, I could speed ahead and create my own line."

COURAGE UNDER FIRE

"My first line wasn't successful. Even though my father was there for me, it was too much for me to handle alone. But with the second line, I understood how much work it would take. If you set goals for yourself, you must make it a priority to accomplish them."

RUNNING THINGS

"Since starting my company, I've learned how to manage people. People want direction, and I have to set parameters, but I also have to hire people who are self-motivated and give them enough freedom. And,

as the boss, I have to provide some of that motivation."

GROWING STRONG

"Before, I hired a lot of freelancers. Now I have 23 employees—a great balance of talent and personalities. I want to have a work environment where people are happy and effective. It takes a lot of time to cultivate that."

GOODWILL HUNTING

"My motto is, 'Declare, and it shall come to pass.' You can't have dreams and wait for them to fall into your lap. You have to be the person you want to be—and start now. If you don't begin the process yourself, you're going to be waiting forever."

MAKING IT HAPPEN

"Do the research and become educated. Give yourself time to learn your craft. You don't have to be an incredible businessperson and prodigy. Make connections and become an intern in the industry you are aiming at. It's a great way to get an inside look."

Clothing designs by Tracy Reese

raffia
crochet
coat w/
bone
charmuese
slip

net blouse

crochet
skirt

cummerbow

candy embroidered
lawn slip w/train

Reese

Design sketches by Tracy Reese

CARLOS WATSON

In kindergarten, Carlos Watson earned the dubious distinction of getting suspended from school 20 times before finally being asked to leave altogether. Fortunately, his parents refused to give up and eventually found an educational environment in which the Miami native could thrive. That change made all the difference in the world. Watson went on to attend Harvard, graduate from Stanford Law School and serve as a White House legal intern. Yet Watson never forgot his early educational challenges, and in 1996, he, his sister, Carolyn, and his best friend, Jeff Livingston, formed Achieva College Prep Services, a company that uses computer software, books and workshops to help high-school students prepare for college. With more than 200 employees, Achieva quickly became one of the nation's top educational-consulting companies—before it was sold in 2002 in a multimillion-dollar deal. Next Watson turned his sights on broadcasting. The 34-year-old is described as one of CNN's brightest new political analysts.

SUPPORT SYSTEM

"Since first grade, I have never forgotten the importance of having supportive people in my life. These people—family, friends, mentors, partners, clergy—ground you, love you, encourage you and fight for you. So I try to be a good son, friend and mentor to others."

WAKE-UP CALL

"My inspiration came while I was in college. One of my favorite political science professors encouraged me to go into business—not just politics. Then, during my senior year, Tony Brown spoke to a small group of students and asked why all the White students were talking about starting their own companies and we—the Black students—were talking about getting a job."

CREATING ACHIEVA

"I started Achieva because I realized the differ-ence that a second or third chance can make in a young person's life. The early lessons I learned from being expelled as a 5-year-old—and being counted out—gave me the confidence to start my own company and chart my own course. It inspired me to want to make a difference in the lives of others."

CASH FLOW

"I got loans from family and friends, then people known as angel investors, and finally, venture capitalists. My angel investors were wealthy individuals who believed in what I was doing."

MAKING IT HAPPEN

"Choose something you believe in, have a great plan and don't be afraid to ask for help. Work with people who are committed, be strict in hiring (one bad apple can ruin the bunch)—and sell, sell, sell!"

DEBRA MARTIN CHASE

Debra Martin Chase knows how to make hit films. As head of Martin Chase Productions, a Walt Disney Studios–based production company in Burbank, California, the Harvard Law School graduate is the only sister in Tinsel Town producing general-market box-office blockbusters. She has 20 projects in development, and in 2004 she produced *The Cheetah Girls*, the television movie based on books by Deborah Gregory. Chase is a businesswoman and a real go-getter, and her success has been the result of her talent, tenacity and timing.

TAKING THE LEAP
"In 1989 I was working as an attorney in the Motion Pictures Legal Department at Columbia Tri-Star, but law wasn't fulfilling. A movie buff, I wanted to learn more about the film business, and when a position opened up to assist Columbia Tri-Star chairman Frank Price, I took a substantial pay cut to learn from him. For a year, I got to sit in on meetings, read scripts and ask questions. My risk paid off when I was hired as director of Creative Affairs."

MAKING MOVES
"A fluke meeting with Denzel Washington led to an offer to run his production company, Mundy Lane, from 1992 until 1995. During my tenure there, we produced *Devil in a Blue Dress, Courage Under Fire, The Preacher's Wife* and *Hank Aaron: Chasing the Dream,* a television documentary that won a Peabody Award and an Emmy. It was while working on *The Preacher's Wife* that I developed a relationship and a subsequent business partnership with Whitney Houston, running her company, BrownHouse Productions. We scored big with a television remake of the Disney fairy tale *Cinderella,* starring Brandy, and later, the film *The Princess Diaries.*"

CHANGING THE GAME
"*Diaries* grossed more than $109 million in domestic box-office receipts. After I'd successfully run several companies, the powers-that-be at Disney recognized my success and offered me my own production deal. Under that deal, I've produced several film and television projects."

PARLAYING THE POWER
"At one point I was receiving every African-American project in town. Though that's the nature of Hollywood, my aim was to make mainstream films based on best-selling books. I chose family- and girl-themed projects because I love them. As a producer, I have the power to influence, so it's important that the messages are positive. The projects I select have to mean something to me."

MAKING IT HAPPEN
"Read books. Talk to people. Attend meetings. Learn as much as you can about the business. The pie is only so big, and I don't care what color you are, people are going to try to keep you out. Inevitably, there will be good times and bad. At the end of the day, however, it's your relationships that will make the difference in your career."

COURTNEY SLOANE

Courtney Sloane has an amazing eye for detail. Perhaps that's why her A-list clientele includes the major players in the hip-hop community and larger entertainment world. Sean "P. Diddy" Combs, Queen Latifah, Black Entertainment Television—they all have her telephone number on speed dial. In 1991 Sloane founded Alternative Design, a New York City interior-design and architectural firm that specializes in commercial and residential interiors that celebrate multiculturalism with contemporary style. Since opening her doors, the 42-year-old design diva has also transformed her business, which has more than quadrupled in recent years. Before her blazing success, however, Sloane had made the decision to take the leap and venture out on her own.

EARLY CAREER GOALS

"When I went to college at Rutgers University, I was interested in design, but I thought, *A Black kid going into design?* It didn't make sense then. Instead, I studied marketing management."

BOUND FOR SUCCESS

"Prior to starting my own business, I worked for Formica—a company that designs and manufactures all types of surfacing materials—in sales and marketing. Formica paid for me to return to school for design training, so this made my transition into the design industry a natural one. When I left my job, I had saved my money so I could take a year off to prepare and focus on my art. Then I was ready to start my own company."

FIRST BIG CLIENT

"I met Queen Latifah 14 years ago in my loft studio, where I would host weekly art and food-tasting events. She attended and told me that one day, when she really blew up, she would hire me to design her house. Three years later, in 1993, she called. First I designed her house, then her office. After music-industry folk saw what I'd done for Latifah, companies like *Vibe* magazine and Bad Boy

Entertainment came calling. Most of my business is from word of mouth."

IMPORTANCE OF TEAMWORK

"I drive the big ideas but I can hardly facilitate them on my own. By the time any one project is complete, I will have collaborated with 50 or more people, including subcontractors, artisans, upholsterers, cabinetmakers, metalworkers and fabric companies. You're only as good as your team is."

INTERNATIONAL RECOGNITION

"My company is working on several residential projects—the highlight is a 15,000-square-foot residence we're doing in Taiwan. This is our first hit outside the United States. Through recommendations of engineers who were part of the project, I interviewed and got the job."

MAKING IT HAPPEN

"Be courageous! Be bold! But don't let money be the sole motivation for getting into business. You must have perseverance, tenacity, a positive attitude—and a strong support base. You also need a certain amount of financial savvy. But more than that, you must believe in and be true to yourself."

ELLIN LaVar

Sometimes you don't choose a career; a career chooses you. Like many little girls, Ellin LaVar started playing hairstylist when she was 9 years old. She was surprisingly good at it—so good, in fact, that family and friends willingly let her create different looks with their hair. By 14 she had a chair in a local Bronx salon, earning her own spending money. By the time the New York City native majored in physiology with a minor in business at Fordham University, she had had a small business, which, through word of mouth, mushroomed into a larger star-studded enterprise. Now she has created a hair-product line. As a businesswoman, LaVar discovered that there's more to hairstyling than simply doing hair.

WAKE-UP CALL

"I had a receptionist who stole $30,000 in checks from my salon and left me $2,000. After I learned she was stealing my money, I changed the way I ran my business. Naive at first, I had to grow up and become a real businessperson— observant and more detail-oriented. I took over my business and used all my savings to get back on my feet."

STUMBLING BLOCKS

"The biggest hardship was being a woman. The second was being a Black woman. I was not treated with respect or perceived as a person who could maintain a business. I had to prove myself. I wouldn't be called for nonethnic photo shoots because it was assumed that I only did Black hair. I have all types of clients. I am trying to get the point across to people that hair is about texture, not about the color of the skin."

SECRET TO SUCCESS

"I always have a plan, and my plan is never fin-

ished. I set goals for myself. To achieve recognition, I had to be out there, exposing my business— through late nights and intense networking, and foregoing a personal life. Also I try to absorb all the information I can. I'm not afraid to ask about things I don't know."

GROWTH INDUSTRY

"My hair-care line is Ellin LaVar Textures. It is going to be an ultramoisturizing line for dry and brittle hair. It will include a shampoo, hair mask, conditioners and a dry-hair-and-scalp treatment. I'll have an oil with vitamins—and all my products will help keep hair supple and healthy."

MAKING IT HAPPEN

"If you love something, stick to it. Be consistent in whatever you do, and pay attention to the details. You always have to think, *Why is mine different? Why would somebody want to use my products?* Separate your business and personal funds. If you don't have enough money yet, start on a small scale."

LISA PRICE

Freelance television and film work was not enough for Lisa Price, who often found herself in between gigs. In the summer of 1993, the 41-year-old decided to turn a childhood obsession with body lotions into a moneymaking franchise. Carol's Daughter, her line of handmade body-care products, includes body butters, bath oils, sea-salt scrubs and hair oils. Price has never taken out a bank loan, doesn't do any advertising and has grown the 26-employee business by reinvesting profits. In 2003 her concoctions made almost $2.3 million in revenue. With her line of homemade recipes, Price has built a base of loyal, happy customers.

MAKING SCENTS (AND DOLLARS)

"I've loved fragrances since I was little. I made my own combinations and added them to drugstore items for my own use—but people asked for them, so I started giving my creams as gifts. I didn't intend to sell them. But when my mom's church had a flea market, I took my products to sell. I sold everything and I made $100!"

FULL HOUSE

"The business started in my home, where my family and I made products in the kitchen and sold them at craft fairs. By 1999 I had 12 employees, a store and a pretty strong mail-order business because of a short article in ESSENCE. It coincided with the birth of my second child, so we had a toddler, a newborn and the telephone ringing off the hook!"

DISCOVERING THE CREATIVITY WITHIN

"Briefly, I wanted to be a singer. I tried the music business, but didn't like it much. Then I became an executive secretary, but didn't like that either, though it paid the bills. I left and became a television writer's assistant. That I loved and thought I'd do television production as a career. But because I was so happy, my creative side came out. When the show was on hiatus, I would play with creams and lotions in the kitchen."

NO LONGER A HOBBY

"I was watching *Oprah* one day, and her guests were women who had started businesses with little or no money. It was then that I realized that mine was a business, not a hobby! I started discovering all the resources—such as wholesalers—that I needed. To open my store, I borrowed $15,000 from my family to take out the initial lease. I was able to pay them back in six months from profits."

ALL IN THE FAMILY

"My husband and I own and run the company together. One of my brothers manages my Brooklyn store; a cousin manages the warehouse and the graphics. Another cousin in South Carolina takes telephone orders. My husband's cousin is my assistant, and my mother-in-law works in the kitchen, where we formulate and 'cook up' some of the products by hand. Then the products are manufactured in a warehouse."

MAKING IT HAPPEN

"Sometimes the right thing to do is not the obvious thing, so you have to be still to hear that little voice. Try not to be perfect. Mistakes are a fact of life. Learn from them."

YOUR ROAD MAP: A BUSINESS PLAN

A business plan is not only key in helping to keep you on track, but it is the best way to showcase your creative ideas. You can contact institutions such as the Small Business Administration (sbaonline.sba.gov) and the National Federation of Independent Business (nfib.com) for guidance on how to pull together that perfect plan. Below are a few tips to get you started.

MAPPING IT OUT: AN OVERVIEW.

You need to thoroughly explain your business venture. The easiest way to do that is to divide your plan into two main sections. The first part should describe the business and the strategies you will employ to market and manage it. You want to convey your excitement in creating it—assessing the competition, developing a marketing plan, targeting customers, finding the perfect location, building a solid management team and hiring the best personnel. The second section—the core of any business plan—spells out the numbers: income, cash flow and balance sheet projections. At the end, add a section that supports your plan and includes résumés of the principals and managers, diagrams, photographs, tables, letters from your existing clientele, credit reports and other documents that will back the viability of your plan.

THE COVER LETTER.

Each time you send the plan to a possible business contact, mail it with a cover letter. Make it brief (about 200 words). It should explain why you are sending your business plan to that particular person. The goal of this letter is to open the door for future negotiations and to show that you are confident, bright, organized and in control of your venture.

SHOW THAT YOU KNOW.

Don't let your potential investor have to guess what your business will be. If you know your venture, show it. If this is a start-up, discuss your product or service in detail. What makes it unique? What industry is it in?

Where does the particular industry fit within the overall business world? Talk numbers: Percentages and dollar amounts provide a bigger and more complete picture than saying "many" or "lots."

YOUR CUSTOMER AND THE MARKET.
Impress the investor with a full account of your research on the market and describe the customer who's awaiting your product or service.

BEATING THE COMPETITION.
Profile your competitors. Discuss their strengths and weaknesses, as well as what you can learn from them. Be fair, but use this chance to indicate how you are going to differentiate from them and outperform them.

WHAT YOU PLAN TO DO.
This is the time to illustrate your market strategy—the techniques you will use to get the best and most cost-effective response. Take some time with this section because a lot of attention should be paid to pricing. Remember, numbers matter to potential investors and lenders.

LOCATION, LOCATION, LOCATION.
Finding the right spot can be a challenge, but if you have a place picked out, persuade a lender or investor to visit. Use photographs, diagrams and blueprints to show it off.

THE TEAM.
Here's that chance to introduce your management team. Highlight every aspect of their experience that relates to your particular business: accomplishments, education, training and tenacity. The key to an excellent team is balance.

WHO WILL WORK FOR YOU.
In this section, describe the type of people you will hire, their values and skills, how much you will pay and what your enterprise will offer— health benefits, the amount of training they will receive and how you plan to handle overtime and vacations.

WHAT ARE THE NUMBERS?
This is the heart of your business plan—the beginning of the second section of your two-part proposal, as mentioned earlier. First, estimate your income statement, which is basically what you think your net profit will be. That's what's left after you subtract your expenses. Second, determine your cash flow for the year. You may have a lot of money at the start of the year, but you want to make sure it will be enough to handle any surprises. Last but not least, include an expected balance sheet— which will help you to predict what your business will be worth after a certain period of time. You also want to illustrate to potential investors the best news about their return on the investment.

20 WAYS TO PROMOTE YOURSELF IN BUSINESS

Consider that for every worthwhile business endeavor there are at least ten other qualified people with the same set of credentials. What can you do to ensure that you will stand out and be recognized? Most people greatly underestimate the importance of business details. Terrie M. Williams, author of *The Personal Touch: What You Really Need to Succeed in Today's Fast-Paced Business World*, tells us that you can stand out among the crowd if you totally embrace and practice these 20 small, but really important, things.

1. KNOW THAT YOUR REPUTATION IS VALUABLE.

Your reputation often reaches people before you do. With that in mind, understand the importance of how you interact with people. Be sincere, be honest, be prepared, be professional, be thorough, be efficient—and deliver.

2. DO WHAT YOU SAY YOU'RE GOING TO DO.

If you can't deliver on time (and reasons for this should only have to do with circumstances beyond your control), then pick up the phone ASAP and say so. And make sure you meet the next deadline you've set.

3. RETURN ALL PHONE CALLS.

If you can't return calls, make sure someone in your organization returns them.

4. TREAT EVERYONE WITH RESPECT AND COURTESY.

A person's position in life should have absolutely nothing to do with how you interact with them. What goes around comes around.

5. BE VISIBLE.

Go to professional seminars, luncheons, receptions, dinners, any kind of gathering of folks. Don't be afraid to attend a function alone. The point is you have to be out there for people to notice you.

6. WHEN YOU MEET PEOPLE, BE MINDFUL.
Look them in the eye, smile, be personable, have a firm handshake and actually be with the individual at that moment. Research studies have shown that people who smile are perceived as more intelligent than people who don't smile.

7. TRY TO DEVELOP A KNACK FOR REMEMBERING NAMES.
People you meet will be flattered if you can call them by name after only a brief introduction. As soon as you meet each new person, say his or her name aloud. Repeat the name in your head several times as you look at the person.

8. BE AN ACTIVE LISTENER.
If you feel yourself becoming bored or distracted, politely excuse yourself.

9. CREATE A "SMALL TALK" NOTEBOOK.
Be creative—even outrageous—but always professional with your ideas. Take a look at your notes before you go to a function, and be ready. Another surefire way to stimulate conversation: Ask people something about themselves.

10. BE SENSITIVE TO BODY LANGUAGE.
Be aware of how you come across to other people during interactions.

11. SEND A FOLLOW-UP NOTE.
When you meet people you would like to stay in touch with, send a note to say hello. Mention a mutual area of interest.

12. GET TO KNOW SUPPORT STAFF.
It costs you nothing to develop these relationships, and when you call a company you want to do business with, there'll be a better chance of being put through.

13. KNOW YOUR PROFESSION.
Stay abreast of all the latest trends and developments in your field. Know who is doing what, where, when and how.

14. PASS ARTICLES ALONG WITH A NOTE.
If you come across something that may be of interest to a colleague, you'll provide a valuable and unforgettable service that they will appreciate. Print small cards with the message "I thought you might find the enclosed of interest," with your name, company, address and phone number.

15. KEEP GREETING CARDS FOR ALL OCCASIONS.
Pay attention to special occasions (honors, appointments and promotions) of business contacts—and stay in touch.

16. WRITE . . . WRITE . . . WRITE.
Send letters to people you want to do business with. Say "I like your work/your style/your recent remarks/your article."

17. GO THROUGH YOUR ROLODEX PERIODICALLY.
Send a hello note to those people you want to remember you. Keep your name and that of your company in front of them.

18. LET PEOPLE KNOW THAT YOU'RE AVAILABLE.
Make it known that you can participate in panel discussions, seminars and various business and charitable activities.

19. SELECTIVELY DONATE YOUR SERVICES.
Nonprofit organizations may be in need of your expertise. Set the stage for people to know who you are and what you do.

20. SAY "THANK YOU."
Remember that people don't have to do anything for you. It's all about developing a winning style and cultivating relationships.

FAMILY ROOTS

"It is a blessing to work with my son. I was a mother by 17. People thought it would derail me and change my future. But my son influenced my decisions, my dreams and my priorities. And today he loves this line of work as much as I do."

—CATHY HUGHES

CATHY HUGHES AND ALFRED LIGGINS

Cathy Hughes's life is a living testimony that with faith and hard work all good things are possible. She went from teenage motherhood and temporary homelessness to heading the largest African-American broadcasting company in the country. Today Radio One is a billion-dollar corporation that employs more than 2,200 people at 70 stations. But back in 1980, when Hughes purchased her first station, funds were so tight that she had to live at the radio station for nearly a year and a half. Enthusiastic and undeterred, the Omaha native rolled up her sleeves and did what was needed to keep the station afloat. At times she wore all the hats—running the business, raising money, planning the future, selling ads and hosting a show herself. From the time he was a youngster, Hughes's "date" for industry functions was often her son, Alfred Liggins III. Not surprisingly, Liggins grew to love the business and currently serves as Radio One's president and CEO. In January 2004, Hughes, 56, and Liggins, 39, launched TV One, a television network.

WAKE-UP CALL

"I would have been content working for other people if Howard University had licensed the Quiet Storm format—which I created—before other stations copied it. I had an idea that was undervalued. That was a wake-up call: to never let anyone else be in charge of my own professional decisions."

LUCKY BREAK

"There was a station for sale, so I put together a business plan. I went to 32 bankers. My thirtieth presentation was to a Puerto Rican woman banker in Washington, D.C. It was her first day on the job, and she said yes."

DRIVING FORCE

"My passion is to communicate with millions of African-Americans and provide them with information that is not normally provided to them in the media. To be Black in America means that most often you will be interpreted through other cultural perspectives, and 99 percent of the time they're wrong. My driving force is to communicate with my people from our perspective."

FAMILY

"It is a blessing to work with my son. I was a mother by 17. People thought it would derail me and change my future. But my son influenced my decisions, my dreams and my priorities. And today he loves this line of work as much as I do."

MAKING IT HAPPEN

"First you have to believe in and embrace your Creator. Second you have to believe in yourself. I had lost my house, my car—some people thought I had lost my mind—when I moved into the radio station. My mother told me to get a government job. If you know in your heart that you can do something, you can do it."

Laila Ali and Johnny "Yahya" McClain

She is a daughter of boxing royalty; he is a son of life's school of hard knocks. But together, Laila Ali-McClain, the youngest daughter of Muhammad Ali, and her husband of four years, Johnny "Yahya" McClain, a former cruiserweight boxing champion, form a formidable one-two punch. Laila is one of the country's top female boxers, and Yahya, through his company, Absolute Entertainment, manages her, along with other boxers, comedians and actors.

Why work together?

Laila: "It was natural. First of all, boxing is so shady, and people want to use my name. We know what the name Ali stands for. I don't approach boxing differently because I am a woman; I feel like I should be in the ring. I am a fighter."

Yahya: "I lived the boxer's nightmare—I was taken advantage of greatly and mismanaged. I care so much about my wife, and I realized that we would be better off if I took over her career so that bad things would not happen to her. Laila is my partner and my best friend. I try to put the best people around her."

The flow

Laila: "There is no separation. We talk about business all the time. We have a good friendship, and everything flows together. But when we want to relax, we get out of town and away from the telephone and our environment. Then we focus on the relationship."

Money and marriage

Yahya: "We understand our position, and we do not let anyone come between us. The key to our success is that money does not affect us or our relationship. Laila was born into it, I never had it, so you cannot threaten me and tell me that I am going to miss it."

The legacy

Laila: "This is a brutal sport. My father did not want me to get hurt, so he did not support me in the beginning, although he never told me not to box. He tried to talk me out of it indirectly."

Making it happen

Laila: "I want to use my celebrity status in a positive way. If an acting role came through that I liked, I would do it. I can also see myself doing a talk show. And I want to show women that they can do what they want."

Yahya: "As far as boxing goes, I am always looking to develop new talent. Our key is planning the work and working our plan!"

THE ROSS FAMILY

Prestige. Drive. Excellence. That's what 70-year-old president and CEO Norma Ross provides to her customers on a daily basis. For 30 years Ross has been garnering excellent mileage out of her family-operated business—Bob Ross Buick GMC Hummer and Ross Motor Mercedes in Centerville, Ohio. When her husband Robert P. Ross, Sr., passed in 1997, the business-savvy widow was determined to stay in the entrepreneurial lane and keep the family's highly successful car dealership thriving. Now Norma, her daughter Jenell, 34, and her son Robert, Jr., 40, are bringing in more sales than ever. Here Jenell speaks for the family.

RIDING HIGH

"Our dealership employs 150 people and operates on a 12-acre site. In 2002 we were ranked number one in retail Buick volume sales in Ohio and number ten nationally out of 2,800 Buick dealerships. We also added another highly profitable franchise—Hummer jeeps—and we are currently constructing an additional building to house the imported vehicles."

SPREADING THE KNOWLEDGE

"As the only African-American female owners of a Mercedes-Benz dealership in the world, we are committed to increasing the awareness of Black organizations that promote and encourage business development. When I was growing up, my parents were always very community-minded."

TEAM EFFORT

"We were blessed to have inherited a good team of 145 employees. Your staff has to feel appreciated in order to grow and be productive. The purpose of owning a business is to be profitable. That takes everybody's effort. We want to provide a great work environment for our employees, whom we view as our extended family. We all work very closely together to accomplish our goal, which is to buy, sell and service great products. Even as we expand, we are extremely careful about maintaining our strong foundation."

WORD FROM THE WISE

"The major obstacle in keeping our business going was settling my father's estate. Family businesses have to plan carefully or they can lose substantial assets to estate taxes. You have to be mindful of how important planning is to the overall goal."

FAMILY VALUES

"Throughout my life I have observed my mother's willingness and determination to succeed no matter what obstacles are thrown in her path."

MAKING IT HAPPEN

"You should not get into any business without short-term and long-term goals. Always reassess them and make room for growth. Faith is what will keep you going."

Left to right:
Jenell Ross, Norma Ross

KENNETH "BABYFACE" AND TRACEY EDMONDS

Grammy Award-winning producer and singer-songwriter Kenneth "Babyface" Edmonds and his entertainment executive wife, Tracey, are partners in love and business. After they wed in 1994, they formed Edmonds Entertainment Group, which includes a television and management division, a music-publishing arm and an independent film company known as E Square FilmWorks. Their first film, *Soul Food*, grossed $43.4 million at the box office, won five NAACP Image Awards and spawned the Showtime series. The couple keep in harmony by allowing their individual abilities to strengthen their partnership. Babyface, 45, focuses on the creative side, while Tracey, 37, serves as the company's president and CEO, overseeing a budget of more than $5 million.

GETTING STARTED

Tracey: "When I graduated from Stanford in 1987, I wasn't sure what I wanted to do. My mom was in real estate, so I got my broker's license and we opened our own real-estate and mortgage company in Orange County, California. I started hanging out in Los Angeles on the weekends and I relocated there. I met Kenny the weekend I moved."

FORMIDABLE PARTNERSHIPS

Kenny: "I met Antonio 'L.A.' Reid in 1981. We formed the R&B group The Deele and produced other artists. We were so successful that we formed our own label, LaFace Records, and created our own stars."

Tracey: "Through Kenny I learned how music publishing works, so I started a publishing company and then a record label. Then Kenny and I started working on music for the *Waiting to Exhale* sound track. Soon after, I came across the script to *Soul Food*, and we formed our film company."

RISKY BUSINESS

Kenny: "With music, you have a lot more control. But there are many more cooks in the kitchen in television and film. Tracey guides the day-to-day operation and deals with the battles as they come up. She's a great partner."

WHAT'S NEXT

Kenny: "I still spend most of my time writing and producing."

Tracey: "We had our first reality show, *College Hill,* on BET, and we just finished two pilots: one for UPN and an animated series for the Disney Channel. We're also working on a follow-up to *Soul Food* for Showtime, and we have a few film projects in development."

MAKING IT HAPPEN

Tracey: "Whatever you do, you have to put the time in and be willing to get in the trenches. You can't just leave it up to someone else to fulfill your vision. There's nothing too big or too small for you to get involved in. That way, no matter how it turns out, you know you gave it your best effort."

GWEN DAYE RICHARDSON

If at first you don't succeed, take a page from Gwen Daye Richardson's book. In the late 1980's her life and marriage were in crisis, and she struggled to keep her firm afloat. In 1989 both her medical-transcription business and her marriage went under. The following year the Houston resident met Willie Richardson, owner of a local air-conditioning and heating company. In short order, Willie became her biggest booster, business partner and husband. Using $200,000 in funds from a venture capitalist, the couple founded *Headway* in 1993, a political magazine with a probusiness approach that lasted for six years. Next they opened Cushcity.com, an online store specializing in African-American books and entertainment products. Today that business that Gwen Daye, 45, and Willie, 56, created includes a storefront as well as the Web site, and generates more than $1 million in sales annually.

GETTING AFLOAT

"I got the idea for our Web site when my 7-year-old daughter, Sylvia, began reading, and I realized there was a shortage of suitable books for her. We started the Web site using capital from *Headway*; the magazine's 10,000 subscribers provided us with a valuable database of potential customers. When Cushcity.com was launched, we sent out a massive amount of e-mail announcements and got 150 orders in the first three weeks. We ran the business out of our home—we didn't need a lot of stock to get started—and when we received orders we'd purchase the books through a Black distributor."

STAYING ATTUNED

"Cushcity.com started as a Black book site. Over time we've expanded our product line to include videocassettes and DVDs of Black stage plays and Christian comedies, which have become our biggest sellers. Now discount retailers like Amazon and Barnes & Noble have saturated the book market. If we hadn't adapted, we wouldn't still be in business today."

THE DREAM TEAM

"I grew up in an entrepreneurial family. My father was a pastor in Virginia and my mother ran the church's day-care center. For us, business was a family affair—all my brothers and sisters worked at some point in the church with our parents. By my second marriage, I was very clear that I needed a mate who was business-minded, like me, but who had different skills and strengths. My husband and I have worked together for 12 years—he handles the technical area while I handle the marketing. If both partners are committed to the same goal, the union can work well both professionally and personally."

MAKING IT HAPPEN

"We are providing a marketplace for our people in the most effective way possible—through the Internet. We've had many growing pains in building our business, but I believe that anything worthwhile requires sacrifice. Over the past several years our growth has been tremendous, even with limited resources."

THE GRAVES FAMILY

In the late 1960's, Earl G. Graves looked across the landscape of emerging Black businesses and burgeoning Black wealth and saw a void. Nowhere was there a forum for the nation's 100,000 African-American entrepreneurs to share ideas or get business advice. His solution? *Black Enterprise* magazine, which he launched in 1970 with a $175,000 loan from the Small Business Administration. Black Enterprise has grown into a company with 100 employees and annual revenues of about $60 million. Yet Graves has never strayed far from his company's mission: to help build wealth for generations of African-Americans through business ownership. And Graves practices what he preaches—his company remains family-owned, with sons Johnny, Michael and Earl "Butch" holding executive positions. Here Butch, who has taken over the day-to-day running of the magazine, talks about his family's success.

SOMBER START

"My father started this business as a result of a tragic accident. He was an administrative assistant to Senator Robert F. Kennedy, and when Kennedy was killed, Dad found himself without a job. Tragedy became a triumph. Having worked with Kennedy, he understood the power of relationships, and he used them to make and grow a business."

RACIAL LEGACY

"Thirty years ago it was unthinkable for certain types of African-American businesses to exist, but we—Black people—went out and started investment banks, became auto dealers, bought franchises. People died for us to have these opportunities."

THE GREAT DIVIDE

"Real poverty is not having the sense or the desire to dream outside your circumstances. The greatest divide in this country is the wealth divide, and if we can help expose people to opportunities and teach them how to build wealth, those other divides will disappear."

MOVIN' ON UP

"The Black Enterprise/Greenwich Street Private Equity Fund is a $100 million fund that invests in minority-owned businesses. And we've got businesses that are tied to *Black Enterprise*—a TV show, radio business and blackenterprise.com. We continue to strive to provide information."

FAMILY LEGACY

"We owe something to the next generation. I make sure that my children do not take anything for granted. My father stressed that you have to do things in an ethical way, be good to people, and if you do, it will come back."

MAKING IT HAPPEN

"In family-owned businesses, you have to have solid personal relationships before entering business relationships. The most successful family businesses are those with a healthy amount of love that allow people to disagree yet not jeopardize the relationship."

Left to right: The Graves Family: Johnny; Michael; Earl, Sr.; Earl "Butch," Jr.

Clockwise from top: The Graves Family: Earl, Sr.; Johnny; Michael; Earl "Butch," Jr.

Earl Graves, Sr.

SHARON MADISON POLK

In 1989 Sharon Madison Polk lost her father, Julian C. Madison, in a murder that remains unsolved. Polk was heartbroken and terrified that she wouldn't be able to continue the legacy of the family business, Madison Madison International, an architectural and engineering company founded by her grandfather and run by her father. But Polk turned her fear into resolve: She was determined not to shatter the firm and became CEO of Madison Madison and M2 International, a project management firm that she and her father launched in 1987. Between both companies, today she manages billions of dollars worth of construction projects.

CLIMBING TO THE TOP

"In 1978 I started out in the lowliest position in the company—as a gopher—and worked from the bottom up. I moved through the ranks from a landscape designer, surveyor, contract administrator and marketing executive to the company's president in 1987. Most of what I've learned in respect to the business, I've learned from working in it."

FAMILY AFFAIR

"Keeping a balanced life is difficult when you own a business. Having a strong support system is very important. Currently I work with my husband, Robert C. Polk, who has been very helpful in the business, and my mother, Mildred R. Madison, who manages my office building. I believe that God is at the center and is the source of all achievements."

GIVING BACK

"I serve on several charitable boards, but the one that is most important to me is the Julian C. Madison Foundation. We provide scholarships for students pursuing careers in engineering and architecture."

NEWEST PASSION

"I have recently launched Long/Madison LLC, a hotel and retail development company, with Sandra Long, former deputy secretary of commerce for the state of Maryland. We're currently working on two proposed hotel projects, a restaurant and a clothing boutique."

WHAT IS WEALTH?

"Being wealthy is relative. Most Blacks are not in the category of wealth as it relates to White America. I think the issue is, 'What do we need to do to actually get to that level?' What's important is to be in a position to help and influence what happens in our community. That's what true wealth is about."

MAKING IT HAPPEN

"Understand what your goal is, visualize it every day, and make sure you have a plan to get there. You have to remember that success is a journey, so once you reach a goal, you have to continue to set others."

CREATE A PARTNERSHIP PACT

Planning to partner with someone in a business venture? In order to avoid future misunderstandings, you'd be wise to draw up a partnership agreement that spells out each person's accountability. Your pact should cover at least the following issues.

• The name of the partnership, the type of business and the date and purpose of the partnership creation

• The contributions (cash, property and/or work) of each person

• A statement of each partner's share of profits and losses, and provisions for taking profits out of the company (often called partners' draws)

• A delineation of each person's management power and duties

• Information on how the partnership will handle the departure of a partner, including buyout terms and provisions for adding or expelling a partner

• Procedures for resolving any future disputes

MAXIMIZE YOUR MONEY

A spending plan lets you know where your cash is going, so you can make adjustments when necessary. Try these money-maximizing strategies.

PROVIDE FOR EMERGENCIES. In case your income is suddenly reduced, build an emergency savings cushion to cover three months' rent, utilities and food. Stash the cash in a money-market or savings account.

MAKE YOURSELF NUMBER ONE. Take 10 percent off the top from each month's earnings and put it away for future investment.

ASSESS YOUR INSURANCE NEEDS. Life insurance is meant to provide for the needs of those who rely on your income. If you are single, with no dependents, a life-insurance policy may not be necessary.

PAY AS YOU GO. Pay credit cards off in full by the due date each month to avoid having to pay interest charges.

Choosing a financial Planner

With so many financial "experts" offering so much advice, how can you tell if the planner you choose is qualified to help you grow your money? Use this checklist in your initial discussion with a planner. Find out:

✔ How long she has been practicing and some of the companies she has represented.

✔ Whether he has experience in areas that are important to you—investment, retirement, insurance, tax or estate planning.

✔ If she's licensed to sell insurance or securities products and if she is registered to give investment advice.

✔ Which types of clients and financial situations she prefers.

✔ If he'll be working with professionals outside his practice—attorneys, tax specialists, insurance agents.

✔ Whether she's paid by commission, salary, flat fee, hourly rate or a percentage of your assets.

✔ The estimated cost of the work to be performed.

✔ If there's a push to market the financial products of the company she's affiliated with.

✔ Whether she provides a written agreement detailing services to be rendered.

✔ Which organizations he's regulated by, so you can check for past disciplinary, unlawful or unethical actions.

Setting up on the web: a checklist

Set your objectives and put a dollar value on them. This approach helps you determine how cost-effective your plan will be in drawing customers to your Web site.

✔ Identify the costs of the site, such as monthly maintenance and updating.

✔ If you plan to hire a Web designer to build your site, get referrals from other businesses who use them. Ask the designers you interview to put you in touch with several of their clients, and check references.

✔ Make sure your site looks great and is easy to use. Have the information structured so that people can easily find what they are looking for. Design it to be user-friendly, where pages open up

without a lot of waiting time.

✔ Make sure you have a computer powerful enough to handle the software you need.

DISCOVER YOUR PATH

No matter where you are in your career—in transition, at a fork in the road or trying to back out of a dead end, you can move upward and outward by getting to what matters. You can invest the rest of your life. Follow these steps to the path of success.

LET GO AND MOVE ON. Many times we hesitate to take steps forward because we can't clearly see our destination.

Sometimes, even if we're not happy with our situation, we might stick with it rather than making a move. Welcome new beginnings, at the same time allowing yourself to feel a sense of loss for giving up familiar surroundings and colleagues.

TAKE STOCK OF YOUR ASSETS. Make a candid account of your interests, skills and abilities. Determine which strengths will help you reach

your full potential. You are a valuable person, and you have lots to offer. All you have to do is recognize your talents and discover where they best fit.

DECIDE WHAT'S IMPORTANT IN YOUR LIFE. Think about what specific kinds of activities are fulfilling. Do you like working with children? Planning events? Identify what appeals to you and why. Then determine how you can do it and

make money. You should enjoy what you do for a living.

NETWORK, NETWORK, NETWORK. Let as many people as possible know about your desires and goals. Spread the word among family and friends, in your professional and faith-based/religious associations and in your sorority or book club. You never know where you'll find your lucky break.

MARKET YOURSELF. Put the best face on yourself through your résumé, cover letter and business plan. Consult how-to books in the library. Carry yourself confidently.

SET GOALS AND TAKE ACTION. Design a time line with small, attainable goals to keep you moving toward that big one. Actions may include doing extensive Internet or library research, attending conferences and arranging meetings with prospective clients or potential investors.

LOAD UP ON RESOURCES. Read books about career planning or seek out a career counselor or coach. Surf sites on the Net, such as the Small Business Administration (sba.gov).

KEEP RECORDS AND FOLLOW UP. Keep track of business contacts. The more organized you are, the more time you'll have to keep moving towards your plan.

CELEBRATE! Reward yourself after reaching each milestone. Saying "Job well done" will boost your confidence and help maintain your momentum. Find healthy ways to pat yourself on the back. A robust spirit and a well-tuned body can only aid you in your quest.

BE PATIENT. Be confident that positive change will come as a result of patience and planning. Believe in yourself, and the world will believe in you, too.

SO YOU WANT TO BE YOUR OWN BOSS—A CHECKLIST

Long before you decide to strike out on your own, begin planning for entrepreneurship. Create your business plan, and check this list.

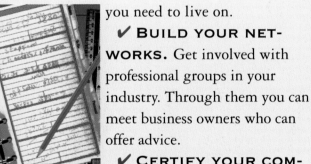

✔ **MAP OUT YOUR FINANCES.** Shore up your credit and savings. Decide on how you plan to finance your business, and identify possible sources.

✔ **KNOW THE FINANCIAL COMMITMENT.** Estimate how much money you will need to put into the business and how much you need to live on.

✔ **BUILD YOUR NETWORKS.** Get involved with professional groups in your industry. Through them you can meet business owners who can offer advice.

✔ **CERTIFY YOUR COMPANY AS MINORITY-OWNED.** To be certified, a company must be 51 percent minority- or female-owned.

✔ **IDENTIFY THE POSSIBLE HURDLES.** Speak to people who have created similar ventures about the challenges they faced initially and what they wish they had known when they started.

WAKE-UP CALLS

"When I finally figured it out, it was almost too late. The only thing that can save you is God."

—MARY J. BLIGE

MARY J. BLIGE

Mary J. Blige had been through years of pain and confusion—child molestation, toxic relationships, destructive self-loathing and substance abuse. Then in 2001 the Queen of Hip-Hop Soul issued a decree: There would be no more drama in her life. And Blige is succeeding. She has emerged victoriously, her psyche and soul intact. Happily married since 2003 to music producer Kendu Isaacs, the talented diva says she feels empowered and at peace for the first time in her life.

LEARNING CURVE

"I didn't know who I was. I was in the music business just making it the best way I knew how. Doing things because I thought it was the cool thing to do. And that's what held me back. It was me being ignorant."

GROWING PAINS

"I didn't know that I was supposed to take care of my business or that my management was supposed to be a representation of me, like a mirror, so to speak. I didn't know that I was supposed to read and be involved in my contractual situation. So that hurt me—the ignorance. When I finally figured it out, it was almost too late. The only thing that can save you is God."

WAKE-UP CALL

"I think the awakening had a lot to do with my meeting Kendu, because he wasn't going for a lot of stuff. I had never met someone who wanted to challenge me like that. Not challenge me in a negative way like, 'I'm going to kick your ass' kind of way. He said, 'You know you deserve better than this. You've got to get your life together.' I didn't want to turn him off. I just started wanting to know more about me and wanting to know more about God."

ATTITUDE ADJUSTMENT

"Selling out, to me, is hating who I am—walking around with a frown on my face just so you can say, 'I keep it real.' The plan is to put a smile on my face for all the blessings that God gave me. Try and get through all this madness with positivity. I plan to be a beautiful woman, a strong woman, a woman that nothing bothers. That's what I'm working on."

IN CONTROL

"I feel more in charge, but I also feel like I know my place. There are certain things I'm capable of doing and certain things I just can't do, like day-to-day management. But everything else that is part of my life and part of my career I'm pretty much ready to take on."

ROLE MODEL

"I see me being an example in getting through my issues so that some other person can say, 'I can do it, too.' I am a leader of a pack of women who need to be free. My biggest thing will be to continue to walk the walk."

MAKING IT HAPPEN

"You've got to use your head in every situation. You've got to figure out what's the best thing for you to do—not what the next person did that you can top. Be smart. People out there are just waiting to eat you up, spit you out. That's what the music business is. Just be strong and sustain."

Left to right:
Kendu Isaacs, Mary J. Blige

MONICA HASLIP

Ten years ago Monica Haslip traded in her marketing gig at Black Entertainment Television for a career that combined her formal arts training and a desire to work with children. Making her dream a reality, the 38-year-old Alabama native bought and renovated an abandoned building on Chicago's South Side and opened the Little Black Pearl Workshop, where inner-city kids ages 10–19 design and sell functional art and furniture. In July 2004, Haslip's vision and revenue expanded. Just five blocks from the original site, the workshop bought a $9 million facility—the Little Black Pearl Art and Design Center—which houses the workshop, a retail store, a gallery and a cyber café.

THE RAINBOW CONNECTION

"I've always wanted to create an entity where children of color could see successful Black artists and learn the connection between art and business. Art has a way of touching people that most of us don't imagine."

WORD IS BOND

"My personal integrity is the most important thing for me in my business. Our organization focuses on doing what we say, with excellence in mind. We serve as examples for the children we work with. They see me, and they think, *She started her business from nothing. If she could do it, I could do it, too.*"

SURVIVING THE LEAN TIMES

"Little Black Pearl's new building cost about $250,000 to renovate. I got the funds from my mom, my own savings and a renovation loan. I committed all my financial resources and I did a lot of the construction work. My effort and energy were focused on bringing that dream to fruition. This experience really took me straight to my faith. I ended up on my knees saying, 'Lord, just show me your will.' "

BALANCING ACT

"We focus on the arts, but the children also come through our door with everything that is going on in their lives. I'm concerned about them, and I tend to take their problems home with me, which can take its toll. To renew my spirit, I meditate, listen to music and travel. And I paint—that's my greatest source of strength and release."

FINDING THE RIGHT MIX

"An organization cannot make it without a strong staff. I hire people who share a passion for the work we do and who bring new ideas to the table. That way we remain innovative and strong."

MAKING IT HAPPEN

"Do something toward your goal every day and recognize that fear and faith don't abide. Plant your feet firmly in faith."

TRACY NIXON

After ten years on the fast track in investment banking, Tracy Nixon found herself putting the breaks on the pressure pedal. She knew it was time to catch her breath and regroup—big-time. As a frequent business traveler herself, the St. Croix native decided to pursue her entrepreneurial dreams of providing an invaluable service: an airport spa where weary travelers could indulge in soothing massages, pedicures, manicures and hair-care services. In 2001, starting with just a small concession in the Indianapolis airport, Nixon, 41, invested her $300,000 savings in the launch of her firm, King Cross Corp. Today the 834-square-foot full-service spa employs a staff of 14.

SEIZING THE MOMENT

"My parents were entrepreneurs. My father was a pharmacist and owned his own stores, and my mother was a nurse who owned an outpatient facility. So when I hit the ten-year mark in my investment-banking career, I knew it was time to investigate other skills buried deep within. I have no regrets about spending ten years in the corporate arena. It has shaped my thinking about employment. Now that I am a business owner, I can see clearly that I enjoy working for myself and being the decision maker."

OVERCOMING THE OBSTACLES

"I first planned to launch an airport nail-care kiosk but had difficulty getting it off the ground. After attending airport-concessions conferences, I sent out introductory letters to concession managers at the 50 largest U.S. airports. It was far more difficult finding a location than I thought it would be. I discovered that securing retail spaces in airports is extremely competitive, so I waited patiently until I found an airport willing to rent me a suitable space. Then I hired a reputable architectural firm to design the prototype."

THE LEARNING CURVE

"I completed an 18-week nail-care course to be a manicurist, learning sanitation and the basics of nail care. That gave me confidence in knowing some of the fundamentals of the new industry I was about to enter."

MAKING IT HAPPEN

"As an entrepreneur, you must clearly decide to become your own biggest fan and supporter. Everyone should experience being an employee as well as being self-employed. Only after having had both experiences can you truly decide which arena best fits your natural inclinations, skills and strengths."

MAGIC AND COOKIE JOHNSON

Although they had been dating for years, basketball superstar Earvin "Magic" Johnson and his wife, Earleatha "Cookie" Johnson, were still newlyweds in 1991, when Magic disclosed that he'd contracted the AIDS virus. This health scare and the public humiliation could easily have signaled the end of their marriage. But the union survived and grew stronger, and their friendship became deeper and richer than ever. With Cookie's support and encouragement, Magic moved into a powerful new phase of his life. Now, more than a dozen years later, he is a successful entrepreneur. His energies have been focused on helping to improve and rebuild inner cities through his chain of movie theaters, Starbucks coffee shops and other business initiatives, which are producing jobs and services nationwide. Magic says Cookie is the inspiration for his postbasketball happiness and success.

HIV AND STAYING TOGETHER
Cookie: "We were at the beginning of a new life together. You come together and you fight together. We just took it one step at a time, which is the only way we could get through it. In order to survive, you have to look to the future. You can't look back or you'll destroy it."

ON LEAVING BASKETBALL
Magic: "The transition was hard, especially since I didn't retire when I expected to. I didn't have to be at practice, and there was nobody cheering anymore. And my ego—I was devastated and an outcast. As a man I couldn't deal with it. I had to rely on the strength of Cookie. I had to rely on my family."

TURNING POINT
Magic: "Cookie said, 'Get your butt up and do something. I'm tired of you sitting here all day. You're driving us crazy. You've got to get out of here. So on Monday I want you to do something.'

When your wife's telling you that, ooooooh! She had never talked to me like that. That's what got me going. And I took off. I started going to the gym every day. I started doing the business things that I had always wanted to do."

FLASHBACK
Magic: "When I was a broke, struggling student, Cookie and I used to sit in the park and I would tell her my dreams and all the things that I wanted to do. And they've come true."

MAKING IT HAPPEN
Cookie: "No matter how busy we are, we always find some time for each other. It's all about bonding and renewing. You have to do that as often as you can. You can't get so caught up in what you're doing that you lose each other."
Magic: "No matter how long it is, we're going to have a ball. Because I believe in living and spreading the joy of life to our cities and our youth."

TRILBY BARNES

In 1991 Trilby Barnes, a self-employed obstetrics nurse in New Orleans, encountered strict government regulations regarding nurses working independently. Because she wasn't affiliated with a nursing agency, Barnes, now 49, was turned down for temporary hospital work. That was when Medi-Lend Nursing Services was born. She started her own agency with $10,000 of her savings, and today Medi-Lend's roster of 2,500 ready-to-hire temporary nurses are in high demand. With a permanent staff of 15, Barnes now has offices in Houston, Texas, and Oakland, and a new division in Baton Rouge, Louisiana. In 2003 her business grossed $8 million. She has turned an early challenge into a stellar achievement.

FINANCING THE DREAM

"My biggest challenge in the beginning was funding. I exhausted all my savings, including the retirement plan I had just started. At first every single dollar I earned went right back into the company."

FINDING HER BALANCE

"Running a business can be a 24–7 undertaking, so for several years I found myself involved in everything but myself. In time, I had no energy left. Last year I shifted my priorities and made a lifestyle change. I cut back to 12-hour workdays and incorporated exercise and good nutrition into my daily schedule. As a result, I have lost 70 pounds, and I find that I have much more stamina."

EXPANDING HER ENTERPRISE

"This year I opened Pro-Lend Staffing in Baton Rouge because I needed to diversify and not depend solely on nursing staff. Because of budget cuts, hospitals are relying on more outsourcing, and they prefer to make one call for all. In addition to supplying nurses, I can offer local businesses a variety of help: janitorial, secretarial, finance or bioengineering. This has pushed my company's annual projected revenues to $9 million."

TAKING ON A CHALLENGE

"The nursing shortage in the United States and around the world is worsening, while the number of individuals in need is increasing every day. According to the National Medical Association, by the year 2020 the shortage in America alone will reach 400,000. Nurses working through agencies such as mine can earn up to $150,000 annually, so it certainly is a well-paid profession. This year my company also sponsored a local Blues and Gospel Run–Walk, raising $70,000 to purchase laptop computers for school nurses."

MAKING IT HAPPEN

"Make everything in your life happen—don't wait for it to come to you. Seek it out and go for it."

PAMELA THOMPSON SMITH

A benign breast biopsy in 2000 inspired Pamela Thompson Smith to create a line of inspirational greeting cards for breast-cancer patients. In 2001 Smith quit her job as publications manager for the Carter Center in Atlanta and used her savings, money-market account and stock investments to create Journey, a line of cards named for the process she feels women go though—from learning about their diagnosis to acceptance and treatment. Smith, a 47-year-old wife and the mother of two teenagers, has sold her cards through ten stores in the Atlanta area and via her Web site, smith-ink.com. She also does freelance writing and editing for corporations, academic institutions and nonprofit organizations.

GIVING BACK

"Although my situation had a happy ending, my cancer scare was a big turning point in my life. I now understand what women diagnosed with cancer go through. Also, as a writer, I wanted to see if there were any greeting cards specifically aimed at women diagnosed with breast cancer. When I discovered there weren't, I decided to craft my own messages."

GETTING STARTED

"Going into business was a difficult decision. When I started my enterprise, my daughter was starting college and my son would be following in four years. My husband and I had set aside money for their education. If I hadn't gone into business, I would have put even more away for them. But I always tell my children to do what they feel strongly about. If it doesn't work, at least they've tried."

DOWN TO BUSINESS

"As a writer, I often worked at home, so I already had my own office equipment. Once I drafted the cards and signed them, I sent them to a graphic designer to fine-tune my rough drafts. When I worked for other companies, part of my responsibility was to put together projects and bid them out to commercial printers. So I treated this as another project, but this time it was my own."

THE CONCEPT

"Every three minutes a woman is diagnosed with breast cancer. I want to give encouragement to women who have this disease and to let them know they are not alone. Also, my cards serve as educational tools. There are breast health tips on the back of each card."

MAKING A PLAN

"Make sure you've assessed your resources and made a time line and business plan to see how far your dollar can stretch. I knew I could get a loan from the bank, but I didn't want to. To start my own business, I kept my own start-up money—which I had saved while I was working—separate from household expenses and my husband's income."

MAKING IT HAPPEN

"A lot of people start their business as a side venture first, which is a great idea. If you feel inspired as I did, pursue your dream."

VICKIE J. LEWIS

As an account manager at a waste-management company, Vickie J. Lewis was downsized from her position in 2000. Her next job, as an independent contractor, compiling data for waste, chemical and environmental projects, allowed her to see that she had enough professional contacts and work experience to have a business of her own. Lewis started VMX International, an environmental-engineering consulting firm that helps businesses in the United States, Canada and Mexico dispose of everything from plain paper to hazardous materials. In its first year VMX snagged major clients and generated $1 million in revenue.

THE TRAUMA OF A LAYOFF

"It was the first time I'd ever been laid off and I didn't want it to happen again. After I was downsized, I worked as an independent contractor for an engineering-consulting firm. My job was to compile statistical data for a project that would transport waste across the country. I'd previously worked in transportation for an airline and a railroad. I thought, *I could do this as a consultant!* Traveling for a year as an independent contractor, I saw how I could do this on my own."

PICKING BRAINS

"I knew a lot about the waste industry, but not about running a business. Networking was not just meeting people, but also about asking many questions. I called professionals in the industry, bounced some of my ideas off them and asked, 'What do I need to do? How did you develop that department? What has made you so successful?' "

SERVICE IS POWER

"I learned that the waste industry is a good old boys' network—and that good old boys' network is real! It's a field run by men, and they want to talk to a guy. But being a woman and a minority doesn't matter to me. It matters that I give good service, and when you give good service, you develop a track record. Then you can go toe-to-toe with anyone and say, 'This is the work we did and this is how our clients rated us.' "

GIVING BACK

"I go to high schools and talk with students about recycling and nontraditional jobs. My husband is a minister, and we tithe to eight different churches. And I just bought a Curves fitness franchise on the northwest side of Detroit. It was part of giving back, because our community had no gym."

MAKING IT HAPPEN

"Put together a winning team that believes in your vision and will work hard. You can't do it alone. Have a good foundation and trust in the Lord. And at the end of the day and on the weekends, have fun and live!"

LIFE AFTER DEBT

Yes, you can get there! Commit to resolving debt issues over a 15- to 24-month period. Here's how to take charge and go from owing money to growing it.

PICTURE PROSPERITY. Visualize your dream financial state. Envision owning your own home, paying cash for a car, going on great vacations, having a comfortable retirement. This prepares your consciousness for wealth.

BE THANKFUL FOR WHAT YOU DO HAVE. Money may be tight, but you still have assets that can help you make more, such as good health, an education and a supportive family. Make a list of positives, including your job, any special skills you can use to earn extra income, items of value you can sell and any savings that might be applied to debts.

STAY FOCUSED. To remind yourself how important it is to get back on track, make another list to show how bad credit has held you back (you couldn't qualify for a mortgage, were forced to pay more for car insurance).

When you're tempted to pull out that plastic, pull out this list.

KNOW THE SCORE. You'll want to review your credit history, find out your credit score and correct any errors. Order reports from the three major credit bureaus: Equifax (800) 685-1111, TransUnion (800) 916-8800 and Experian (888) 397-3742. If you've recently been turned down for credit, you're entitled to a free copy of your report. Web sites such as consumerinfo.com or myfico.com can give you access to information from all three companies.

ASSESS THE BIG PICTURE. Dealing with denial will empower you. Use the credit report to map out all your debt, including credit-card and student-loan balances. Don't forget to account for any sums owed to friends and family.

TRACK YOUR EXPENSES. A budget will be your best friend and isn't hard to draw up. Keep track of all expenses for a month. Then review how much was spent on needs (groceries,

rent, gasoline) versus wants (designer clothing, a fancy dinner out). The idea isn't to omit the latter category; just look for cheaper thrills (trade outfits with a stylish friend, learn to make soufflé at home). Commit the money saved to erasing debt.

TACKLE ONE DEBT AT A TIME. Unless you've chosen to consolidate all your debts with one credit institution, put the bulk of your bill-paying money toward your worst debt—the one with the highest interest rate—and continue paying the minimums on the rest. Contact each creditor and tell them how much you can pay toward the balance each month. Most will be willing to work with you.

DON'T GO IT ALONE. Help is available if you need it. A nonprofit credit-counseling agency may be able to help.

DEBT DISTRESS:
THE WARNING SIGNS

If you find yourself with more credit- and charge-card bills than you can comfortably pay, you may be suffering from debt distress. But if you recognize the symptoms, there are steps you can take to get the situation in check. Consider these warning signs and remedies.

YOU DON'T KNOW HOW MUCH YOU OWE UNTIL THE BILLS ARRIVE.
If you usually owe more than you thought, begin tracking each expenditure throughout the month by writing down the date, purpose and amount.

YOU REPEATEDLY PAY BILLS LATE. At least pay the minimum on time. Otherwise you will not only incur a late charge, but your account will be reported to the credit bureaus. And a bad credit report can block approval for a car loan or home mortgage.

YOU OFTEN CAN'T MAKE A MINIMUM CREDIT-CARD PAYMENT. Try to keep credit-card payments at about 10 percent of your monthly net income. If your payments exceed that and you can't make them, get consumer credit counseling to help manage your debt.

IT TAKES 60 TO 90 DAYS TO PAY OFF BALANCES THAT YOU USED TO PAY IN 30. The longer you take to pay off balances, the more interest costs you'll incur. Ask your credit-card provider to lower the interest rate, or transfer the balance to a card with lower rates.

YOU FREQUENTLY EXCEED YOUR CREDIT LIMIT. Always keep track of how much credit you have left. You are charged an over-limit fee when you exceed your account's credit limit, and you may not realize it until your statement arrives.

YOU USE CASH ADVANCES TO PAY BILLS. Save these for emergencies. With cash advances, you pay a higher interest rate, there is no interest-free grace period and there is usually a transaction fee.

For help with debt problems, log on to myvesta.org or call (800) 680-3328.

Sharing the Wealth

"**A**s you give, you receive. I have had people who gave me guidance and taught me a lot. That's what motivates me to help others."

—GRANT HILL

GRANT AND TAMIA HILL

Grant Hill, six-time NBA All-Star, and his wife, R&B singer Tamia, share more than a marital partnership. The couple, who married in 1999, are committed to sharing their time and wealth with others. Despite ankle injuries, Hill, 32, is signed to a seven-year contract with the Orlando Magic. Tamia, 29, made her professional debut on Quincy Jones's 1995 album *Q's Jook Joint*, and in 2004 released a new album. The couple has used a mix of entrepreneurship and charity to help enrich their lives and the lives of others.

PURSUE YOUR PASSION

Grant: "I am blessed to be able to do something that I love. I started playing basketball when I was 7 years old, and I have been fortunate enough to continue that into my adult life. I have had people who gave me guidance and taught me a lot. That's what motivates me to help others."

Tamia: "I started to sing in church when I was 6 and realized at a young age how powerful music is. I was 17 when I got my first record deal in 1992."

MO' MONEY

Grant: "We try to diversify and make our funds grow. There's not a lot that can prepare you for signing a $45 million contract when you're 20, and I've made mistakes. We try to live comfortably, but not spend foolishly. I am aware of every penny we spend. I formed my own company, Hill Ventures. Whether I build a strip mall, an office building or residential property, I plan to develop real estate in the next chapter of my life."

GIVING BACK

Grant: "As you give, you receive. Tamia and I have funded two Habitat for Humanity homes. And we love African-American art. We have a 45-piece art collection that we've sponsored to expose children to this part of our culture. All proceeds from a book about the exhibition go to arts education in schools, in addition to a $10,000 scholarship program."

SPREADING THE WEALTH

Grant: "I made a $1 million donation to my alma mater, Duke University, to establish the Grant and Tamia Hill Scholarship Endowment Fund for athletic scholarships and a $50,000 donation to prevent child abuse. I also set up the Calvin Hill Scholarship Endowment Fund at the Duke Divinity School in honor of my father, the Malcolm McDonald Scholarship Fund at Dillard University in honor of my grandfather, and the Grant Hill Achiever Scholarships in Orlando and Detroit for undergraduate studies."

Tamia: "Once you have success, you are able to change people's lives."

MAKING IT HAPPEN

Grant and Tamia: "We've all been blessed with special gifts and talents. You just have to find something that you enjoy doing and define what success means to you."

RUBEN STUDDARD

Ruben Studdard is more than our American Idol—with a voice that captivated millions and a persona that captured our hearts. Although he's affectionately nicknamed the Velvet Teddy Bear, there's nothing playful about his vision and drive. Since winning the national talent competition in 2003, the 25-year-old Birmingham, Alabama, native has recorded a best-selling album, handed out scholarships and drummed up support for historically Black colleges. Despite his being the relatively new kid on the block, it's over the long haul that Studdard hopes to make an impact on the lives of others.

REACHING BACK

"I am trying to do big things. In 2003 I started my own record label, Real Music Records. I have two inspirational artists and a rapper from Chicago. We also have the Ruben Studdard Foundation for the advancement of children in the music arts. Right now we are trying to broaden our scope so that we can help buy instruments and other materials for kids at inner-city schools. We are giving out our first scholarship—$5,000—for a kid who is planning to go to school and become a music major."

PUSHING BLACK

"Because I had the Black college experience, I want to raise awareness about the rich culture and academic support that Black colleges and universities offer. We are doing a tour to enlighten Black communities about educational and career options—to open their eyes to the opportunities available to them."

KID CONNECTION

"I have worked with the Pick and Roll Foundation, which was started by basketball star Kenny Anderson. We travel to different cities, where we meet and interact with kids to motivate and encourage them."

REGARDING FAME

"Fame hasn't changed me or the people around me. I don't get down like that. But I've never worked so much in my life, never had such a busy schedule. I am blessed. I try to stay humble."

FUTURE PLANS

"I hope that in the next five years Real Music Records will be a $5 million company and that the foundation will have touched the lives of millions. I plan to be around for a long time and to make a lot of music."

MAKING IT HAPPEN

"Stay focused, and always be prepared, because you never know when your opportunity will come. You have to be ready. I have always wanted to sing, so when the opportunity to appear on *American Idol* came along, I just did my thing. But I made sure that I was prepared."

Nawal Nour

As a Sudanese teenager, Nawal Nour always knew that she would become a doctor to heal people. But it wasn't until Nour discovered that a few of her loved ones had endured the cultural practice of female genital circumcision that she began researching this ritual of her native land and other African countries. Today she is the founder and director of the African Women's Health Practice at Brigham and Women's Hospital in Boston, the only facility of its kind. In 2004 the 37-year-old Brown and Harvard graduate was awarded a MacArthur Foundation grant for her devotion to expanding health-care services for circumcised immigrant women.

FIRST PASSION

"I went into medicine because I was interested in addressing women's health issues. Initially, I was interested in women's rights issues and getting into law, but I decided on medicine because it focused on global women's issues."

A CAREER CALL

"Living in Sudan and Egypt, I became aware that my friends and some of my cousins were circumcised. I began reading voraciously about the condition. I didn't think I'd make a career of it, but I knew it was an issue that touched me. I'm passionate about women's getting the best health care and not having to endure the scrutiny of providers who focus only on the circumcision and often give less than optimum care. My goal is to educate the general public about female circumcision without its being sensationalized by the media."

MASTERMIND

"When I was doing my residency in obstetrics and gynecology, women of African descent started coming to see me because they knew I was an African doctor who understood the cultural aspects of female circumcision. Gradually I built a small practice for these patients, and once I completed my master's in public health at Harvard University, I approached my chairman at Brigham about the need to formalize the practice for African women. We were able to start it as a pilot project, and it succeeded."

COMMUNITY OUTREACH

"My work is my passion. Not only do I take care of patients, but I also conduct outreach reproductive workshops where circumcised African women can get together and discuss their experiences in the United States and learn about how to talk to their physicians about other important issues. At the end of the workshops, I feel that I've been able to translate a message of empowerment to these women, which is incredibly fulfilling."

MAKING IT HAPPEN

"It's really important to follow your passion, but it helps to have a great support group and good mentoring. You can't always do it alone. Sometimes people have ideas, but without groundwork, those ideas can fail. Make a needs assessment. Before jumping in on your own, always do your homework and talk to those who have experience."

FINANCIAL AND INVESTMENT LINGO

You don't have to know a debenture from a derivative to secure your financial future. But by familiarizing yourself with the following terms, you'll enhance your investment savvy.

ACTIVELY-MANAGED MUTUAL FUND: A mutual fund in which the fund manager actively tries to outperform the market by buying and selling individual securities to shape the overall fund portfolio.

AGGRESSIVE-GROWTH FUNDS: Stock mutual funds that seek high growth through aggressive investment strategies, and these funds generally buy stocks of emerging companies that offer the potential for rapid growth.

ANNUITY: An investment in which the policyholder pays a lump sum or makes installment payments to an insurance company and receives income at retirement.

ASK: The lowest price at which an investor is willing to sell a security.

ASSET ALLOCATION: The distribution of your investment funds across categories of financial assets, such as stocks, bonds, money-market accounts. Spreading your investments among various sectors helps offset the possible risks and rewards, based on your future investment goals.

ASSET-ALLOCATION FUND: A mutual fund that typically includes a mix of stocks, bonds and cash equivalents. This type of fund allows you to diversify among classes with one investment. Over time, fund managers reallocate the fund's assets based on changing market conditions with the objective to keep the asset allocation percentages steady.

ASSET CLASS: A broad categorization of an investment. The main asset classes are stocks, bonds and cash equivalents.

ASSETS: Any item of monetary value owned by an individual or company, such as real estate, stocks or bonds.

AVERAGE MATURITY: The lifetime of a bond, ending when the final payment of that obligation is due.

BALANCED FUNDS: The objective of these funds—which purchase a mix of bonds, preferred stocks and common stocks—is to preserve the initial principal and income as well as provide long-term growth of both that principal and income.

BEAR MARKET: A period of falling stock and bond prices.

BID: The highest price at which an investor is willing to buy a security.

BOND: Long-term debt security sold by a company or government agency, with a specified interest rate and fixed due date for interest and principal to be paid. Interest is usually paid every six months and its face value returned at maturity. The minimum denomination is $1,000, with $1,000 increments thereafter.

Types include:

Corporate Bond: Debt sold by corporations as an alternative to offering stocks. They're riskier than government securities and offer higher interest.

Mortgage-backed Bonds: Bonds that derive their income from a pool of mortgages and are issued by agencies such as Fannie Mae, the largest U.S. mortgage financier.

Municipal Bond: Issued by a state or municipality, municipal bonds (also called "munis") are exempt from federal and, in some cases, state and city taxes.

Treasury Bills, Notes, or Bonds: Government debt that is sold through the Treasury Department. Since they are backed by the full faith and credit of the federal government, they are considered virtually free from risk of default.

Zero Coupon Bond: Bond sold at deep discount from its face value, with no period interest payment.

BROKERAGE ACCOUNT: An account with a brokerage firm that holds your investments and allows you to buy and sell securities.

BULL MARKET: A period of rising stock and bond prices.

CAPITAL APPRECIATION: The growth of your investment's principal.

CAPITAL GAINS OR LOSSES: The difference in value between what you originally paid for an investment and the price at which it was sold.

CASH ACCOUNT: A brokerage account that requires you to pay for trades in full by the settlement date.

CERTIFICATE OF DEPOSIT: A deposit in a bank for a specified period with a guaranteed interest rate.

CHURNING: Excessive trading in your account by a broker in an attempt to rake in big commissions. While difficult to prove, churning is illegal under the Securities and Exchange Commission's rules.

COMMISSIONS: Fees paid to a broker for executing trades.

COMPOUND INTEREST: Interest that is computed using the principal balance plus the previously earned interest. Compounding measures the growth of an investment when dividends or appreciation are reinvested.

DEBENTURE: A debt secured solely by the borrower's integrity.

DEPRECIATION: A decline in an investment's value.

DERIVATIVE: A security whose worth is largely derived from the value of another underlying security or benchmark.

DISCOUNT BROKER: A broker that sells and purchases securities at low commission fees.

DIVERSIFICATION: Spreading an investment over a large number of securities—such as stocks, bonds and cash equivalents—to reduce risk in that portfolio.

DIVIDEND: The distribution of a company's earnings to shareholders, and typically paid to you in cash or stock.

DIVIDEND REINVESTMENT: An investment plan that allows shareholders to automatically reinvest cash dividends and capital gains distributions into additional shares of the company's stocks.

DIRECT STOCK-PURCHASE PLAN: Investors can purchase shares directly from a company, thus avoiding brokerage fees.

DOLLAR-COST AVERAGING: An investment strategy of purchasing securities—usually mutual funds—in fixed dollar amounts at set intervals, aiming to lower the average cost per share over time. This tactic does not assure a profit and does not protect against losses in declining markets.

INDEX: A statistical composite that gauges changes in the economy or financial markets, or that is used as a benchmark that economic or financial performance is measured against. Some market indexes include the Standard & Poor's 500 Index, Dow Jones Industrial Average, NASDAQ Composite Index, Consumer Price Index and Russell 2000.

INDEX FUND: Mutual funds that attempt to match returns of a market index. When investing these funds, you are seeking to "buy the market" and not outperform it.

LIMIT ORDER: An order to buy securities and commodities at or below a specific maximum price, or sell them above or at a specific minimum price.

MARGIN: Buying securities from a broker with borrowed money. It allows you to purchase certain securities using the assets in your account as collateral for the loan.

MUTUAL FUND: An investment company that pools money from shareholders and invests in a variety of financial assets, such as stocks, bonds and money market assets. A mutual fund stands ready to redeem its shares at the current net asset value, depending on the total market value of the fund's investment at the time.

NET ASSET VALUE: The total value of the assets owned by a mutual fund, minus all liabilities, divided by the number of shares outstanding.

NET WORTH (WEALTH): Total value of assets minus outstanding debts.

PORTFOLIO: An array of investments held by an individual or organization.

PRIMARY MARKET: The market where investment bankers first sell new securities.

PROSPECTUS: A legal document issued by mutual funds offering securities or mutual fund shares for sale. The prospectus will provide information about the manager's specific goals, fees and practices of the fund.

SECONDARY MARKET: A market where investors buy securities from other investors, rather than from an investment bank.

SECURITIES: Investment vehicles such as stocks, bonds and money-market instruments.

TAX-DEFERRED INCOME: Earnings on an investment account that are not taxed until withdrawal.

VESTED: The percentage of ownership in a retirement-plan assets.

VOLATILITY: Fluctuation in the value of an investment within a short period. The more volatile an investment is, the higher its risk and potential return are. Volatility is usually measured by calculating the annualized standard deviation of daily change in price.

YIELD: The annual rate of return on an investment paid in dividends or interest, expressed as a percentage.

TAKING STOCK

Planning to jump back into the stock market? Add these terms to your investment know-how.

BLUE-CHIP: Common stocks of companies that have a long history of stable earnings and/or growth in dividend payments, and considered the least risky.

COMMON STOCK: A unit of ownership in a public corporation that entitles owners to vote for directors and receive dividends from the company's growth.

DOW JONES INDUSTRIAL AVERAGE (DJIA): A composite measuring the performance among the collection of "30 blue-chip" stocks traded on the New York Stock Exchange (NYSE).

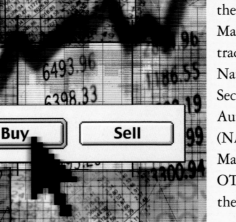

EARNINGS PER SHARE (EPS): A company's earnings, also known as net income or net profit, divided by the number of shares outstanding.

GROWTH STOCK: Shares of a company that is in an expanding industry and has the potential to continue growing over time. While in the long-term growth stocks usually outperform average stocks, they are more risky than average stocks because of their higher price/earnings ratios.

INITIAL PUBLIC OFFERING (IPO): The first time a company makes its shares available for sale to the public.

MARKET CAPITALIZATION: The total value of a company's stock. For instance, a company with 50 million shares outstanding, selling for $15 a share, has a market cap of $750 million.

OVER-THE-COUNTER (OTC): Refers to stocks that are not listed on one of the major stock exchanges. Many OTC stocks are traded through the National Association for Securities Dealers Automated Quotations (NASDAQ), National Market System (NMS), OTCBB (Bulletin Board) or the Pink Sheets.

PENNY STOCK: Low-priced stocks that are usually traded for less than $1 a share and issued by speculative companies with a short or sporadic revenue and earnings history.

PRICE-EARNINGS RATIO (P/E): Price of a stock divided by its earnings per share. A high P/E may suggest that a stock price is too high.

STOCK EXCHANGES: Three major U.S. institutions where stocks are traded: NYSE (New York Stock Exchange), NASDAQ (National Association of Securities Dealers Automated Quotation), and AMEX (American Stock Exchange).

FOUNDED IN FAITH

"**W**ith every generation, God leads his people into change or proposes some-thing that they have not seen before."

—MICHAEL FREEMAN

Michael and Dee Dee Freeman

Married life was bleak for Michael and Dee Dee Freeman as twentysomething newlyweds. After five years of struggling, the couple turned to God for help in fixing their relationship. And in the process, Michael, a policeman at the time, began laying the foundation for a ministry. The Spirit of Faith Christian Center in Temple Hills, Maryland, is now a multimillion-dollar organization with a shopping plaza operated by its members. Through their ministry, the Freemans share what they have learned about marriage to help troubled couples find their way back to joy. And through church businesses, they've created opportunities for members to benefit via jobs and fellowship. With a devoted congregation of 7,000, the Freemans are proving that families who pray together stay together.

Seeing a vision

Michael Freeman: "After making a mess of my life and marriage, I surrendered to God's will and He unveiled to me the concept of creating businesses for the church community. Although I felt a little hesitant about doing it, it has been successful. Now other churches are buying minimalls, and there's a new breed and generation of pastors who aren't accepting traditional ways of doing things."

On a mission

"I'm a fourth-generation pastor, so it's in my blood. However, I didn't see a concrete way to tap into business opportunities with ministries until I discovered an abandoned shopping center in Temple Hills, Maryland. The church bought the property for $825,000 in 1995 and added $3.3 million to transform the run-down strip mall into a spiritual and commercial center we call Faith Plaza. It has a hair salon, bookstore, upholstery store, nursery, arcade and computer training center. When I left my Dad's church, there was the feeling that you couldn't mix business with church affairs. I believe that what Christians are buying Christians should be supplying."

City of God

"We are in the process of creating Faith City. We will have a place for battered women, drug-rehabilitation programs, a theater, as well as clothing stores, a library and residential homes."

Making it happen

"With every generation, God leads his people into change or proposes something that they have not seen before. Find talented, motivated, loyal individuals who will help you carry out your mandate."

PERNESSA SEELE

As an immunologist at Harlem Hospital in the 1980's, Pernessa Seele saw first-hand how AIDS patients were forced to suffer alone because of the stigma associated with the disease. In 1989, determined to remind African-Americans of our responsibility to one another, Seele approached Harlem churches about openly addressing HIV and AIDS. Her plan: a week of prayer for the sick. Seele's Black Church Week of Prayer was so successful that it has become an annual event and the largest AIDS-awareness program in the African-American faith community. In 1999 Seele started Balm in Gilead, a nonprofit corporation that helps 15,000 churches in America and Africa educate their members—some 200 million congregants—about AIDS. Now, by joining forces with Christian and Muslim leaders, she hopes Balm in Gilead's Africa HIV/AIDS Faith Initiative can help end the devastation in the motherland, which has already taken 13 million lives in the past decade; more than 28 million now live with the virus.

GETTING STARTED
"When I became an immunologist, I thought I'd be a research scientist, but when the AIDS epidemic hit, my degree in immunology and my expertise was suddenly in demand. So I became one of the first AIDS educators in New York. I got a job at Harlem Hospital as an AIDS administrator."

FILLING A NEED
"I was born in the all-Black town of Lincolnville, South Carolina. I thought the church people in Harlem would respond like church people in Lincolnville, by going to see people who have AIDS. I knew that there were 350 churches in Harlem, but few of the church members were visiting AIDS patients. That's when I got the idea to mobilize a week of prayer. If you say 'prayer,' Black folks say 'okay.' That allowed the faith folks to have a conversation about the disease. They were hungry for some way to deal with the crisis."

GROWING AND GOING GLOBAL
"In 2001 the Centers for Disease Control (CDC) asked us to expand Balm in Gilead to Africa. We are the only African-American organization to get CDC funding to mobilize the faith community on that continent. So far we've brought our program to five countries: Ivory Coast, Nigeria, Kenya, Tanzania and Zimbabwe. We're learning how positive it is when African-Americans and Africans work together, because they usually see only Whites—not African-Americans—come to help."

MAKING IT HAPPEN
"Often we believe we have a calling, something we really need to do, and we struggle with it. But it comes down to two things: Either you do what you believe you are supposed to do, or you struggle for not having done it."

FLOYD FLAKE

In Queens, New York, he's known for community building. In Washington, D.C., he's known as a former congressman. In the world of academia he is known for serving his alma mater, Wilberforce University, the school he now heads. Floyd Flake, the 59-year-old father of four, is a clergyman for the new millennium. He believes that it's his job to minister to his congregation's earthly concerns as well as their spiritual needs. He has brought senior-citizen housing, schools and single-family homes to the St. Albans, New York, community where his church, Greater Allen AME, is located. Flake, who accepted the call to ministry at age 15 and graduated from Ohio's Paine Seminary, also studied business and once worked in Xerox Corp.'s marketing department. For this maverick, dedicating himself to the ministry was more than just a calling. Determined to make a difference, Flake has changed an entire community built on faith.

BUILDING THE CHURCH

"I spent two years at Northeastern's business school, but in 1976 I was called to serve as pastor of the Greater Allen AME church. Before long I was able to develop the church into a major corporation with 11 subsidiary corporations, funded through tithes and offerings. That money we raised, leveraged with federal, city and state programs, made ours the second-largest church in the AME organization."

NEW-FASHIONED RELIGION

"We have taken a traditional church model and grown it into a $34 million company. We got started by building senior housing, the first of 300 units. We also realized a need to emphasize education, so we opened a pre-K-through-eighth-grade school. Once we got the school up, we began to purchase properties within a 26-block radius of the church. We built 161 homes and sold them to first-time buyers. While all this was going on, the church was growing and flourishing. We built a $23 million cathedral for worship and have just finished a $42 million senior–assisted-living project."

MESSAGES FOR ALL

"I was always engaged with the people in prayer while working for Congress. I never dropped the mental part of my faith. I still managed to teach Bible study—I just changed the hat."

TEAM FLAKE

"Allen Christian School was the vision of my wife, Elaine. The school is in its twentieth year, and our test scores equal those of the highest-performing districts in Queens. Elaine is copastor of the church and directs the ministry when I am traveling. Our chief financial officer handles the businesses and other operations."

MAKING IT HAPPEN

"People need to look for the power within themselves and seek to fulfill whatever their dreams are. You cannot be satisfied with one accomplishment."

FAITH-BASED BUSINESS

I never think of my company—Inner Visions Institute for Spiritual Life Coaching—as a purely business venture. It is the part of my life that I offer to God. Everything I do for God, I do in love. This is what works for me.

LOVE WHAT YOU DO, AND DON'T DO IT FOR MONEY.

I love to write, to teach and share my ideas and to support others in finding their passion and vision in life. It may not be a sound business principle, but believe me, it works! Love magnetizes whatever it touches, and it attracts more love to it: Love and money are ruled by the same vibration.

HAVE A VISION, AND STAY FOCUSED.

When times were real tight, nothing I did generated an income. I was tempted to throw in the towel and go back to practicing law. But alone at night, I would remember why I got started: loving people, sharing information, healing the planet. When I'd wake up in the morning, I would be so charged up, I'd renew my vow to do whatever was neces-

sary to spread the word.

MAKE YOURSELF UNIQUE.

Dennis P. Kimbro, Ph.D., author of *Think and Grow Rich: A Black Choice,* gave me the best advice I have ever had, which I

still use today: "Don't try to do everything. Specialize! Pick something and stick to it. Do what you do in such a way that people must have what you are offering."

—IYANLA VANZANT

STARTING YOUR OWN NONPROFIT

If your passion is helping others, you can start your own nonprofit organization. Getting a not-for-profit agency up and running is not as difficult as you may think. If this is an effort you want to launch, this checklist will help when you are ready.

ARTICLES OF INCORPORATION. Start by filing Articles of Incorporation with the Office of the Secretary of State to legally establish your nonprofit's name and purpose.

BYLAWS. Write a specific set of bylaws for your nonprofit that will define how it will be managed, which duties the officers, staff and board members will have and how those responsibilities should be carried out.

TAX-EXEMPT STATUS. If your nonprofit is charitable, educational, scientific, literary or religious, you can establish tax-exempt status under sections 501(c)(3) of the Internal Revenue Code, enabling you to solicit tax-deductible contributions.

BOARD OF DIRECTORS. First, decide what you want board members to do. Raise funds? Help with legal work? Get media coverage? Then make a list of potential candidates from diverse backgrounds. And when you approach them, be honest about what you'll expect them to do.

MISSION STATEMENT. Craft a mission statement in a few sentences that communicates exactly what your not-for-profit organization intends to do. Look at a successful model, but differentiate in some way to make your business unique. Research organizations that have similar missions.

BUDGETING. Think realistically about your potential expenses. How much will it cost to rent space, pay utilities, purchase or lease equipment and hire staff? It may be more effective to operate from your home until you get sufficient funds.

FUNDING. Many nonprofits survive on grant money alone, and corporations and foundations are your best bets. Follow their application guidelines.

NETWORKING. Political connections can be helpful. By supporting your cause, they can help make building your nonprofit from the ground up a lot easier.

PROFIT FROM YOUR TALENTS

If you love doing something, why not try to make it profitable? Build on your business skills. Attend a seminar or class that will help you to start putting things together. Here are a few tips.

- *What is your talent?* Rediscover that hobby you never have time for anymore. Grandma taught you to knit? Get started on those hats and shawls you'll sell for the holidays. Make greeting cards. You've been braiding hair for years—start charging.

- *Branching out.* Set yourself up. Maybe you can start with a home-based business. Define your skills: accounting, calligraphy, personal coaching, dressmaking, baking, cooking, organizing services, storytelling, pet sitting, résumé writing, tutoring, wedding planning, cleaning services.

- *For the long term.* Consider how to grow your budding business. Give it a name. Hire an assistant. Expand your customer base. Tell everyone about your product or service. Solicit orders from neighbors or the stores in town.

PHOTOGRAPHY AND ART CREDITS

INDEX